GARDEN POOLS

FOUNTAINS & WATERFALLS

Tall horsetails surround this tranquil koi pond (see page 49).

Water lilies add a burst of color to the pool's surface. For specifics on growing them, see page 50.

Book Editor
Scott Atkinson

Coordinating Editor
Suzanne Normand Mathison

Design
Joe di Chiarro

Illustrations
Lois Lovejoy
Rik Olson

BY POPULAR DEMAND...

Garden pool technology has taken a great leap forward in recent years. Enthusiasm for water gardening and raising koi have also reached new heights. For these reasons, we decided that the time was right for an up-to-date book on the subject.

We begin with a planning overview, which includes many color photos of contemporary pools, fountains, waterfalls, and streams. The next two chapters focus on water plants and fish, respectively. Finally, we present pool-building and maintenance specifics, including the latest information on liners and shells, masonry, pumps and plumbing, and outdoor lighting.

This edition has benefitted greatly from the input of many professionals in the field. We'd especially like to thank Paul Cowley of Potomac Waterworks, Michael Glassman of Environmental Creations, and Herb Simons of U.S. Koi Sales for reviewing the manuscript and generously offering their expertise. Fred Tonai of Golden State Fisheries also read parts of the book and provided numerous suggestions. We are also grateful to the many home owners and garden pool lovers who shared with us their knowledge of and enthusiasm for pools, plants, and fish.

Special thanks go to Rene Lynch for carefully editing the manuscript and to Marianne Lipanovich for scouting photo possibilities.

Cover: Murmuring, man-made brook feeds a serene garden pool; a small pump recirculates the water. Native boulders and border plantings tie the scene to the surrounding landscape. Landscape architect: Bob Royston. Landscape contractor: John Nishizawa Co., Inc. Cover design by Susan Bryant. Photography by Tom Wyatt. Photo styling by JoAnn Masaoka Van Atta.

Photographers: Ray Albright: 21 bottom; Scott Atkinson: 56; Derek Fell: 14 right, 15, 25 center; Richard Fish: 42 top; Audrey Gibson: 36 bottom left. Mark E. Gibson: 2, 24 center, 25 right, 36 right, 50 left. Harry Haralambou: 24 right, 36 top left, 48 left; Pamela Harper: 18 top; Saxon Holt: 8 bottom, 18 bottom, 20 bottom, 46, 48 right, 49 right, 58, 64; Horticultural Photography: 7 top, 24 left, 50 right; Jack McDowell: 10; Michael McKinley: 4, 6, 7 bottom; Stephen Marley: 21 top, 30 top; Don Normark: 32 bottom; Jeff Stone: 3, 25 left; Michael S. Thompson: 12 left, 44 bottom right; Tom Wyatt: 1, 8 top, 9, 11, 12 right, 13, 14 left, 16, 17, 19, 20 top, 22, 27, 28, 29, 30 bottom, 31, 32 top, 33, 34, 37, 38, 39, 41, 42 bottom, 43, 44 top and bottom left, 45, 49 center, 61.

Photo styling: JoAnn Masaoka Van Atta: 1, 8 top, 9, 11, 12 right, 13, 14 left, 16, 17, 19, 20 top, 22, 27, 28, 29, 30 bottom, 31, 32 top, 33, 34, 37, 38, 39, 41, 42 bottom, 43, 44 top and bottom left, 45, 49 center, 61.

VP, Editorial Director, Sunset Books:
Bob Doyle

16 17 18 19   QPD QPD 02 01

Please visit our website at
www.sunsetbooks.com

_1 & 22_

CONTENTS

Handcarved lion head spills water into a wall fountain's holding pool (see page 25).

GARDEN
POOLS

If anything in nature can be called magic, it must be *water*. The shimmer and sound of water have cast their spell throughout history. The Chinese, and later the Japanese, perfected the balance of three basic elements: water, stone, and plants. The Romans used fountains and stair-step pools to cool hot summer nights along the Mediterranean. The English Victorians built palatial homes for goldfish, and the French spread out enormous sheets of water in front of their chateaux.

Quiet and reflecting, dancing and image-shattering—water still brings both energy and old-world charm into a garden. Whether it reflects the sky and clouds, a piece of garden sculpture, or the arching branches of a nearby tree, a garden pool presents an ever-changing picture. The cooling effect of a fountain or waterfall on hot, dry summer days and evenings is as welcome as in Roman times. Goldfish or koi dimpling the surface of a fish pond continue to be a captivating sight. For gardeners, a water garden opens up a whole new world.

Autumn Reflections
Quiet, reflecting water is special, as any gliding duck knows. Though this one is obviously large-scale, such ponds provide ideas and inspiration: with careful planning your garden pool, even if it is a fraction of the size, can evoke a similar mood.

Although few of us have the space or inclination to build a full-scale, traditional pool, water can play a part in many other ways in today's landscaping scene. You can choose from among three basic possibilities: a small accent pool, a formal pool, or a natural or informal pool. Today's do-it-yourselfer also has a choice of materials—from traditional concrete, stone, and brick to easy-to-install liners and shells. In addition, there's an entire realm of pumps, filters, and lighting hardware. Here's a closer look, in words and pictures, at the many possibilities for today's garden pool.

Water as a Decorative Accent

Water in small amounts serves an ornamental purpose in a garden, and it doesn't take much effort or expense to achieve satisfying results. Let the pool draw attention to arrangements of container plants as seasonal blooms appear, or start a tiny water garden (for pointers, see "Tub Gardens" on page 10). Or accent the pool itself, placing a glass float or colorful bloom on the water's surface. The simplest "decoration" of all is to keep the water clear and let birds play in it.

If you want to start small, there are tiny decorative garden pools that have the advantages of being both portable and versatile. You can pick them up at garden supply and statuary stores. Innovative garden decorators have demonstrated that almost any container capable of holding water can—with suitable cleaning and appropriate placement—become an attractive accent pool. Add your own ideas to the following list: bonsai bowls, terra cotta planters, wine barrels, industrial drums, claw-foot bathtubs, laundry basins, cattle-watering troughs, and hot water (or other) tanks. Scout around your house and yard (or grandmother's) for that chipped enameled dishpan, rusty wheelbarrow, or galvanized bucket; you may even find a crock still gathering dust since Prohibition days.

Want to create your own accent pool? Consider freeform concrete—shaped, colored, and textured to resemble a waterpocket in native stone—or a sandcast circular basin. Waterproofed lumber or marine grade plywood can also fit the bill. Leave the basin in its rough state or paint it, tile it, or line it with a mosaic of pebbles, seashells, or whatever you have available.

Starting Out Small

A tiny accent pool, such as this gracefully aged birdbath, is one of the simplest ways to introduce water to your garden. Most feathered bathers prefer 1 or 2 inches of water. Garden of the Heyward-Washington House/The Charleston Museum, Charleston, South Carolina.

Formal Garden Pools

In a Victorian garden the pool was frequently a generous circle, oval, or rectangle, slightly raised, set in the center of an area, and surrounded by spacious walks so that it could be viewed from every side. But the Victorian garden failed to survive the disappearance of the patient, pipe-smoking professional gardener with quarters above the coach house. A few gardens are still large enough to accommodate such pools, but in most cases the pool has to be set near some border if there is to be enough room for anything else.

If you build a pool of concrete, brick, stone, or tile in a simple shape, you'll succeed in recalling the old style. Classic rectangles or ovals are best and can be scaled up or down to fit the available space and harmonize with the surroundings. Fountains and sculpture are characteristic accessories.

Formal pools can be raised above ground level, semi-raised, or sunken, depending on the site and the border effect you wish. A raised pool takes the most effort and materials but provides surfaces for sitting and sunning, as well as for container plants and decorations.

Formal pools look best when set in formally landscaped areas with adequate elbowroom. Crowding a formal pool into a small area tends to destroy vital esthetics that depend upon proper scale.

Natural Pools

A natural-appearing pool is almost any body of water without square corners, perpendicular walls, or man-made edges in sight. It should have native stone and soil close around it, along with plants common to the area in which you live.

Traditional Ties

For centuries, formal pools like this one were the norm for any proper European garden. To continue the tradition, plan a circular or rectangular shape, either sunken, raised, or semi-raised; careful plantings emphasize the formal pattern. Butchart Gardens, Victoria, British Columbia.

Hidden Garden

This classic octagonal pool is the central feature in a circular garden enclosure visible only from the edge of the main garden. Water lilies are among the few water plants appropriate in both formal and informal settings. Design: Thomas Church.

From that point, the variety of choices open to the designer is as wide-ranging as the designs are beautiful. Yours could be an alpine pool, a willow-shaded pond, a tiny spring at some desert oasis, or a water retreat such as one you remember from a vacation. Japanese gardens are an excellent source of natural ideas and techniques.

Most older natural pools are hand-packed shells of reinforced concrete; today, do-it-yourselfers may opt for pool liners or fiberglass shells (see pages 12–13). It's the border that counts: typically, edges are camouflaged with lush plant materials or rocks, soil, and other material so that the pool appears to be the work of nature.

A natural-appearing pool is the most enjoyable to create, but it's also the most demanding. The physical construction is not the difficult part, however; the problem is finding a way to artfully blend your chosen materials.

Unlike formal pools, informal designs seem to fit comfortably in limited space. However, a boulder-framed pool requires ample elbow room. Boulders fill up space quickly, so the shell of the pool itself has to be sizable to remain in scale.

For do-it-yourselfers, the only rule is this: Keep it simple. Complex designs not only are difficult to manage during construction but also rarely achieve the hoped-for effect.

Peaceful Retreat

Waving water irises, an arching bridge, reflections of drifting clouds—the Japanese garden tradition has inspired countless garden pool designs. If you're planning a natural pool, visit nearby public or private gardens where you can shop for ideas. Hakone Gardens, Saratoga, California.

Nature Adrift

A natural pool is usually best for mixed plantings and fish. Yellow flag iris and pickerel weed frame this quiet scene, while water lilies and fish share the water rights.

Locating Your Pool

Finding the right location for a garden pool is not always a simple matter. An obvious spot, it seems, is where everyone can enjoy it. If such a location requires renovation of your entire yard, though, it is obviously impractical. Don't hestitate to look beyond the backyard: consider a dramatic entry pond with arched bridge; a quiet sideyard setting outside the study window; an enclosed courtyard pool with lush plant life; even a living room koi pond.

Before you begin, you'll need to check any deed restrictions, setback requirements, and local ordinances that may affect the placement of your pool. Bone up on local building codes as well. Then you'll need access to the site for supplies and any earth-moving equipment; if plumbing and electrical connections are required, make sure they're nearby.

If you are planning to add plants or fish (see page 11), consider the pool's location in relation to the sun. The site should be protected from wind and situated away from deciduous trees that will rain a steady supply of leaves and twigs into the water. Drainage is important: *don't* choose a low-lying or "bottom" area that will constantly overflow in wet weather. Water seeks its own level, so if you can't provide a level site, you'll have to build a retaining wall at one end or design a split-level pond, connected by a waterfall or stream.

Front-yard Water Garden

As this entry pond attests, a garden pool needn't be tucked into a backyard corner. Complete with cascades and native boulders, the entry not only creates a unique water environment for the owners but presents a dramatic view for approaching guests. Brick and aggregate in the bridge and walkways tie the pool environment to the house. Landscape designer: Dennis Tromburg/Zierden Landscaping.

Valley Oasis

Tumbling natural falls and a large holding pool (which doubles as a swimming pool in season) create a cool retreat for a hot summer's day; stepping stones lead the way. Tender ferns, rhododendrons, and drought-tolerant valley oaks share the scene; drip irrigation system and mini-sprayers help keep moisture lovers green without wasting water. Landscape designer: Dennis Tromburg/Zierden Landscaping.

TUB
GARDENS

If you don't have space for a full-scale water garden, don't despair—instead, plant a tub garden. You'll need only a few springtime hours and some simple ingredients: a suitable container, a sunny site, gallons of water, some bog or aquatic plants (you may have to order these ahead from a specialty catalog), and a few fish to help keep the pool clean.

The container. Searching for the right container is half the fun of tub gardening. If you want a good-size pool, buy at least a 25-gallon container, or build your own; almost any leakproof vessel will do. A wooden half-barrel is an attractive choice, and it's easy to find. For a more ornate pool, use a large decorative tub, such as the one shown in the photo at right. You can always place the main container inside a more handsome—but less seaworthy—barrel or tub.

The site. Because a water-filled 25-gallon container is heavy (over 200 pounds), it makes good sense to set up your water garden in its permanent location. You may prefer to place it on garden ground rather than on a deck or patio: the pool will have to be drained occasionally, and there's always some chance of seepage.

As you evaluate possible sites, remember that it's important to provide plenty of sunshine: most aquatic plants need at least 4 to 6 hours of full sun daily. Keep in mind, too, that your water garden should complement its surroundings; you may want to locate the pool where it will reflect color from blooming trees and flowers, for example.

Sunshine, a small container, and a few water plants are all you'll need to begin tub gardening. Design: Aerin Moore, Magic Gardens.

Filling and planting. Before placing a wooden, metal, or unglazed ceramic container in its permanent location, it's best to coat the inside with epoxy paint or to line it with PVC plastic. A dark-colored coating makes the surface more reflective.

With the exception of plants that simply float free on the water's surface, root aquatic plants before placing them in the pool. Plastic pots are best, since they hold up better than clay when submerged in water. Fill pots with garden loam; an inch-

thick layer of sand at the top of each pot helps keep soil particles in place.

Submerge planted pots in the pool, usually positioning them so pot tops are 6 inches or more under water. A few plants do best if containers are only partially submerged; see the listings on pages 52–55. To raise plants to the proper height, set up pedestals made from bricks or overturned pots on the pool's bottom.

Add a goldfish or two, or some mosquito fish, to keep the water free of insects; don't overfeed fish, since this could disturb the pool's ecological balance. A tiny fountain jet, driven by a submersible pump, provides visual interest as well as oxygen.

Once a year, drain the pool and scrub it out thoroughly with a mixture of four parts water to one part household bleach.

Possible plants. Listed below are a few popular water plants. For more complete descriptions and planting details, see Chapter 4, "Water Gardens."

Arrowhead (Sagittaria latifolia)
Cardinal flower (Lobelia cardinalis)
Horsetail (Equisetum hyemale)
Lotus (Nelumbo)
Japanese iris (Iris ensata)
Pygmy cattail (Typha minima)
Umbrella plant (Cyperus alternifolius)
Water hyacinth (Eichhornia crassipes)
Water hawthorn (Aponogeton distachyus)
Water lily (Nymphaea)

Honored House Guests

Something's fishy about the living room shown below—the koi pond, to be exact. Part of a family room remodel, it's plenty deep (about 30 inches) for energetic fish. The construction is concrete, with mortar-embedded stone; the rocks on the bottom are loose to facilitate cleaning. At right, the owner feeds koi from his hand, showing how well these pets have taken to their indoor lifestyle. Landscape contractor: John Nishizawa, Co., Inc.

Plants or Fish?

Before attacking the backyard with pick and shovel, take time to consider the special needs of water plants or fish, if they're to call your garden pool home.

Planning a water garden. Water plants add new colors, shapes, and textures to a garden, especially the hardy and tropical water lilies, oxygenating plants and grasses, and floating plants such as the water hyacinth. A "bog" or border garden adjacent to the pool, receiving some overflow or oversplash, creates a special environment, perhaps with bright blue and yellow irises or papyrus catching the sunlight.

If you want plants in your pool, as you almost certainly will, you'll have to make some design choices. Most plants require at least 4 to 6 hours per day of sunlight, so a sunny site is the number one prerequisite. You'll also probably want a ledge or shelf about 10 inches deep and wide around the pool edges, perfect for many submerged water plants. If you're thinking of raising fish, too, you may wish to build a divided pond, or erect some other type of barrier: fish think nothing of rooting your favorite water plants into oblivion.

For details on choosing and growing water plants, see Chapter 4, "Water Gardens."

Planning for fish. If you're considering the acquisition of a few goldfish or koi, beware! You're almost certain to get hooked and want more. Common goldfish are the patriarchs of ornamental fish; many fancier breeds, suitable for outdoor pools, have come from them. Colorful koi are carp, not goldfish. Larger, spunkier, and longer-living than goldfish, they are known for their outgoing behavior and affection for their owners.

Fish prefer a bit more shade than is optimum for plants, which also discourages the formation of algae. Pool depth is critical: a koi pond should be no shallower than 18 inches and ideally between 24 and 36 inches, or even deeper. It should have shallow places for feeding and fish-watching and deeper water where the koi can go when surface water heats up or starts to freeze—or to escape a raccoon or the family cat. Don't use rough stone below the waterline, because fish can be injured by rubbing against the edges.

A koi pond requires more careful planning than a pool with plants only or no plants; this will almost certainly require some form of pump for aeration and a filtering system for battling ammonia and other impurities in the water. For details, see pages 15–16. If you need additional help with pond design, or with selecting and raising fish, turn to Chapter 5, "Goldfish & Koi."

Pool Materials

At one time, packed bentonite clay and stone were the only choices for a sturdy garden pool. Although many formal pools are still built with masonry materials—concrete, brick, tile, and stone—today's do-it-yourselfer has two handy alternatives: pool liners and fiberglass shells. Here's an introduction to all the commonly used pool materials. You'll find complete installation instructions in Chapter 6, "Building Your Pool."

Flexible liners. These are the big news in garden pools, and you'll find some type of liner in virtually any mail-order catalog. They are not the thin, brittle polyethylene sheets from the hardware store but much stouter sheets—20 to 30 mils and thicker—designed especially for garden pools. Stock sizes range from about 4 by 5 feet to 23 by 30 feet (finished pool size is somewhat smaller); special sizes and shapes may be special-ordered. Installation is straightforward: basically, you dig a hole, drape the liner over the inside, and fill with water. The typical black color allows for maximum water reflectancy; you won't see the liner itself.

PVC plastic is the standard liner material, but it becomes brittle with exposure to the sun's rays. Life expectancy is roughly 10 years. More UV-resistant—but twice the price—are industrial-grade PVC or butyl-rubber liners. Some pool builders prefer EPDM, a roofing material, available in 10- to 40-foot-wide rolls and .045- or .060-inch thicknesses. Most liner materials can be cut and solvent-welded to fit odd-shaped water features.

Fiberglass shells. To picture these fiberglass pool shells, think of a spa or hot tub buried in the ground and filled with plants and fish. They're the easiest pools of all to install; you simply shape a hole that matches the shell's outline, lower the unit into place, and backfill while adding water.

Most shells are treated with gelcoat, a spa material that comes in several colors (again, black usually looks best). A reasonable selection of shapes and sizes is available, but many are too shallow to house fish. Some prefab units can be joined to make larger units; there are also fiberglass streams and waterfalls. Price is about four times or greater than for a comparably sized PVC pool; life expectancy is 20 years plus (although gelcoat is often warrantied for

Easy-to-install Fiberglass
Preformed fiberglass pools are available in a variety of shapes and dimensions and are among the easiest units to install. You can either leave the rolled edges exposed, as shown, or hide them with overhanging rock borders or plantings. Design: Peter Chan.

Riverstones
Ever-popular stone adds the riparian look to this small natural pool. The base of most stone pools is poured concrete or gunite; the stones are then secured in a thin bed of mortar. Landscape designer: Paul Reed.

Dressing Up with Tile

Tile is a sure-fire way to introduce tradition and elegance to your garden pool. This pool doubles as a working spa, with poured-in-place gunite shell and concrete walls capped with hand-painted Spanish tile. Tile inlays in the Mexican paver border echo the cross-shaped motif. Landscape architect: Jeff Stone Associates.

1 year only). Fiberglass shells are available at some garden centers and through mail-order catalogs. Be sure to figure in shipping prices: transporting a large, noncollapsible shell can be quite expensive.

Concrete. Poured concrete has its evident advantages. It is the most plastic of materials, as well as the most impermeable. Its utilitarian character can be disguised with paint or a facing of brick, tile, or stone, and it can also be plastered for greater texture or water protection. The material is normally reinforced with steel to withstand the pressures of soil and water. The amount and size of the steel depend on the geographical location and the structural requirements.

Freeform concrete can be stacked to a slope of about 45 degrees with ordinary mix and can be made steeper with an air-sprayed, professionally applied mixture called gunite or shotcrete. For crisp, perpendicular angles and perpendicular walls, you'll need carpentered forms and poured concrete (see pages 72–73).

Concrete does have some material disadvantages. It is heavy to work with, and forms, if required, can be time-consuming to manufacture. Concrete also demands considerable post-construction care: the surface must be kept damp for at least a week to allow it to cure. Also, concrete contains lime that has to be neutralized before fish or plants can live in the water.

Concrete blocks sometimes do the job better: their greater size means quick assembly and fewer mortar joints per square foot of surface than other masonry units, and they can be faced with tile, a stone design, or even brick. Concrete blocks are easier to reinforce than brick because of their hollow cores.

Brick. The ruddy face of brick is a warm and familiar friend in both formal and informal gardens. A raised pool with brick walls provides a traditional home for water lilies, goldfish, and koi. Brick serves equally well in a modern context. Brick-in-sand patios with sunken pools appear regularly in contemporary surroundings.

But amateur bricklayers can come to grief with bricks if they use them to form the walls of a pool, as they are too porous to do the job unaided. Some homeowners use poured concrete to form the shell and then face the above-grade portion with brick, or they mount a brick rim atop the concrete walls of a sunken pool. You can also use brick to cap or cover a plastic liner—achieving, in effect, the best of both worlds.

Borders & Edgings

Often, it's the border around the pool that makes or breaks your pool's appearance and harmony within the garden in general.

Your border treatment partially depends on whether your pool is raised or sunken. Sunken pools need some kind of raised border to keep groundwater from running into the pool during rains. In a pool without a drain or overflow, runoff can drown plants near the pool and float fish over-board with fatal consequences. Even with a drain, the pool water will probably be muddied by inflowing groundwater. A border an inch or two above the ground helps prevent all these things.

A gravel-filled drain all around the pool will take care of water drainage along the surrounding surface. It's a good idea to also hook up an overflow pipe from the pool to the border drain.

When you come to edging materials, the choice is broad: a grass lawn; an adjoining bog garden or rock garden (often piled against a partially raised pool, or used at one end of a sloping site); native stones and boulders; flagstones laid in a mortar bed; a wide concrete lip (especially useful as a mowing strip if grass adjoins the area); brick laid in sand or mortar; redwood or other rot-resistant wood laid as rounds or upright in columns; terra cotta tiles; or railroad ties.

Everything in Its Place

A foreground spa, twin garden pools, and a swimming pool (not shown) all nest efficiently in this backyard scene. Wood decking ties all the elements together and provides a walkway for a leisurely stroll. Landscape architect: Michael Kobayashi/MHK Group. Additional design: American Landscape, Inc.

Ideas for Edgings

The world of these koi carp is circumscribed by four border materials: upright logs, a simple wooden bridge, flagstone paving, and native stones for accent.

The Inner Works: Pumps, Filters & Hardware

Small garden pools may maintain a relatively stable environment (see "Pool Ecology," at right) on their own after an initial start-up period, but large fish ponds, waterfalls, and fountain units require some basic hardware. Here's a discussion of the components you might need.

Pumps. A pump serves three basic purposes: (1) It recirculates water to a fountain or over a waterfall, conserving water and providing the pressure or "head" necessary to pull or push water through the plumbing system; (2) It allows you to drain the pool in the event of a leak or for routine cleaning and maintenance; and (3) It helps aerate water, adding oxygen and promoting clean water for fish. You'll need a pump to power most pool filters.

Pumps have two basic types: *submersible* and *recirculating*. The best submersible pumps are made from brass and stainless steel; housings coated with epoxy resin are also popular. These pumps are designed for low-volume, part-time use, such as driving a small fountain or waterfall.

Large volumes of water and a constant demand—such as a biological filter system (see below)—favor a recirculating pump housed outside the pool. Don't buy the swimming pool design; it's overly powerful and gobbles too much electricity. Instead, look for a *circulator* pump, which moves a higher volume of water at a lower pressure. Adding a strainer basket ahead of your pump's inlet helps keep leaves and other debris out of the pump itself.

For details on pump ratings and installation, see pages 80–81.

Filters. Filters for garden ponds run the gamut from simple strainer baskets to swimming pool filters to custom biological filters for large koi ponds. The three basic types are chemical, mechanical, and biological.

Chemical filtration simply means utilizing algicides and other water-clearing agents to attack particular impurities. This is often the method of choice for a small garden pool that has no plants or fish.

Mechanical filters use some type of straining mechanism to trap dirt particles in water passing through. One variety simply circulates water through a box or cylinder containing activated carbon, zeolite, brushes, or fiber padding. While these devices are economical, they tend to clog easily under heavy service (as in a fish pond), requiring frequent backwashing and/or replacement of the filter media. Most catalog models can be powered with a simple submersible pump.

"Why is the pool water pea-green, and what can I do about it?" The answer to this frequently asked question requires a short lesson in pool ecology.

When water gardeners speak of a "balanced" pool, they're referring to the ecological balance. *Algae* is the villain in green; a balanced pool is one in which the growth of algae is controlled naturally. Floating plants, oxygenating plants, and some assorted pool critters are the good guys.

Acting in direct competition for sunlight (on which algae thrive), floating plants such as water lilies keep water cool and clear. Small fish feed on algae and on insect larvae, keeping the mosquito problem around your pool to a minimum. Garden pool catalogs promote water snails as algae nibblers (though some pool experts feel they're more trouble than they're worth).

Owners of koi ponds have one additional concern: the build-up of toxic ammonia, which is excreted by fish. The key to grappling with ammonia lies in the *nitrogen cycle*. What this means is that successive stages of bacteria break down ammonia into *nitrites*, then into *nitrates*, which are much less toxic to fish and feed plants and algae—which in turn nourish fish. Biological filters are designed to promote the growth of helpful bacteria. Aeration via a waterfall, fountain, or some other means helps provide critical oxygen to both bacteria and their larger poolmates, the koi.

Clean water provides a happy home for a portly bullfrog. Floating plants, oxygenating plants, and critters work together to keep a pool free of algae and insects.

More efficient is the pressurized swimming pool filter; of the three major types—cartridge, diatomaceous earth (DE), and pressurized-sand—the sand filter gets the highest marks from experts. These filters do require regular backflushing, in addition to a change of sand (120 pounds or so) periodically.

A *biological* filter is a variation on the mechanical theme, relying on pumped water to circulate down or up through a filtering medium. The difference is that the filter bed supports a colony of live bacteria that consume ammonia, converting it into nitrates for use again by plants and fish. The system depends on constant aeration to keep the bacteria alive (without sufficient oxygen, they can die in as little as 6 to 8 hours); a recirculating pump—and perhaps an emergency air pump—is in order.

Other hardware. Need to keep a constant water level in your pool? Install a float valve, either a special pool model or the toilet-bowl type. When the water level sinks below a certain level, the valve opens and fresh water enters the pool. Another useful device for a large pool is a swimming pool skimmer, which is typically poured into place on the side of a concrete pool.

To run a pump or pool lighting (see below), you'll need a nearby outdoor 120-volt receptacle, protected by a ground-fault circuit interrupter (GFCI), which immediately shuts off power to the line in the case of an electrical short or power leakage. Also, don't forget an inside switch to run the pump for a waterfall or fountain, or to control light fixtures.

Installing a drain in your pool provides for easier maintenance. The lack of a drain means the pool has to be siphoned or pumped empty for cleaning, so the last water puddles will be hard to flush from the floor of the pool.

Lighting Your Pool

When it comes time to light up your garden, you have a choice of standard 120-volt or low voltage as well as a choice of surfaced or submerged pool fixtures.

Because they're safer, more energy efficient, and easier to install than standard 120-volt systems, low-voltage lights are often used outdoors. Such systems use a transformer to step down standard household current to 12 volts. Although low-voltage fixtures don't have the "punch" of line-current fixtures, a

State of the Art

Here's a koi pond, a waterfall, and a biological marvel all rolled into one. The twin pools (the upper one is shown at left) are concrete faced with fieldstone. Below the gravel bottom of each pond is a biological filter; below the filter system is what the owner calls the "submarine" or control center (see the photo below). A German recirculating pump keeps the entire show in motion. Landscape architect: George Girven & Associates. Landscape contractor: Anthony Bertotti Landscaping, Inc.

A Quiet Glow

An illuminated bridge over the water leads the eye and lights the way to the gazebo in the background. The lights are 120-volt, submersible pool fixtures. They shine through glass blocks embedded in the bridge—some squares were sand-blasted clear, others left opaque. Architect: Mark Hajjar. Pond consultant: Paul Cowley/Potomac Waterworks.

little light goes a long way at night. But the standard 120-volt system still has some advantages outdoors: the buried cable and metallic fixtures give the installation a look of permanence, and light can be projected a great distance.

Outdoor surface fixtures range from well lights and other portable uplights, to spread lights that illuminate paths or bridges to downlights designed to be anchored to the house wall, eaves, and trees. Downlighting is tops for pinpointing special garden features; uplighting is good for accenting or silhouetting foliage. Low-voltage halogen MR-16 bulbs are popular for accenting; PAR spotlights, available in both low and standard voltage, are best for a wider light pattern, both in and out of water.

Most underwater lights are designed to be recessed in a concrete pool wall. You can also purchase portable lights with lead plates that keep them on the pool or stream bottom; move these about to accent a waterfall or plantings. Fountain units often come with their own integral lighting schemes, sometimes with optional filter kits for changing colors. For more on these, see pages 86–87.

What's best, submerged or surface lighting? It's a matter of taste. Surface lighting can be adjusted with more subtlety and precision; also, fish and plants tend to look best when illuminated from above. On the other hand, brash underwater lights produce dramatic effects, and they can be fine-tuned with a dimmer switch.

Rainpocket

A tiny reflecting pool mirrors an overhanging tree fern; the "rainpocket" is freeform concrete, hand-shaped and "weathered" to resemble mountain granite. Design: Harland Hand.

Formal *and* Casual?

Nestled into a terraced backyard landscape, this sunken accent pool combines a contemporary outline with natural surroundings. Boulders, ground covers, and nearby railroad tie steps furnish the natural look; poured concrete aggregate paving creates the clean, modern pool outline.

One Step at a Time

Visitors cross this entry pool on poured concrete "islands." Water appears to flow continuously through the house, but there are really three adjacent systems, beginning with the entry pool. A self-contained stream section picks up inside and seems to exit through a back wall into the waterfall shown on page 37. Landscape designer: Michael Glassman/ Environmental Creations.

Life at the Beach

An existing stream provides the input for this backyard pool, the focal point of an extensive owner-built natural landscape. A small background dam helps form the pool, which is lined with 30-mil plastic; the fountain and waterfall are driven by a submersible pump. The plantings are about half "found" native species and half purchased. The owners added sand to make the foreground "beach." Design: Bill & Caroline Furnas.

Persian Art

The pool, bubbler fountains, and cascades add an exotic look to this Seattle landscape, with lighting as a 20th-century touch. Landscape architects: Talley, Boughton & Takagi.

Floating Deck, Japanese Style

A garden pool enclosed in an inner courtyard provides a tranquil, private space that delights from inside, too. An effective way to make a pool look larger is to cantilever a deck a foot or two over the edge, giving the impression that the water extends beyond.

The Swimming Pool Gone Wild

Today's swimming pool increasingly does double duty as a natural water feature. This pool sports an informal shape, complete with boulders, border plantings, and an upper pool with a waterfall. Swimmers can savor the waterfall from an underwater ledge, or cross a bridge to the raised deck, spa, and firepit. Design: John Withers, Master Pools by Geremia.

Desert Oasis

Defined by the brick edging and rear retaining wall, this semi-circular, sunken pool makes a subtle statement at one end of the wooden deck. The substructure has a poured concrete base and concrete block walls, and it is faced with tile, standard brick, and stabilized mud adobe bricks in the back. Landscape architect: Richard William/Oasis Gardens.

GARDEN FOUNTAINS

Water in motion is nearly always dramatic, and a flowing fountain introduces water as a star performer in the garden scene. But in addition to merely entertaining with a colorful show, a fountain does more practical work. During the hot, dry days of summer, it fills the air with moisture, providing a cool garden retreat for you, your family, and guests. The musical sounds of a fountain also help wrap the area in privacy, screening off outside noise and distractions.

Contrary to popular notions, most contemporary fountains are *not* water guzzlers; in fact, many are not hooked up to water supply lines at all. A submersible or recirculating pump recycles the pool water and feeds it back to the fountain head or water inlet, where it's used again, again, and again.

Fountains that spray, fountains that spill, and fountains that splash are the three basic types. Versatile spray fountains have fountain heads that send water upward in shapes ranging from massive col-

Wall of Water

Surprise! Fountains do not issue only from the mouths of frogs or milk maidens' jugs; this one was built into a concrete block and stucco wall when the house was constructed. The steep fountain ramp is lined with Saltillo pavers; water is recycled through a recirculating pump. Landscape architect: Deweese/Burton Associates.

umns to sprays as delicate as lace. Spill fountains take two basic forms: either simple tiers of spill pans or more elaborate wall fountains. Splash fountains can contain either sprays or spills, but only in a splash fountain is water interrupted by a piece of sculpture.

Various fountain heads and spray or spill fountains can be purchased directly from the manufacturer or from garden supply, plumbing, and hardware stores, as well as some mail-order catalogs. Wall and splash fountains, on the other hand, are nearly always custom designed, either by the homeowner or by a landscape architect.

The Spray's the Thing

Basically, a spray fountain uses water in opposition to gravity, sometimes for picturesque water patterns, sometimes for interaction with sculpture, and, on occasion, simply for the sight and sound of falling water.

Choosing the spray pattern. With a little help from an array of available fountain heads, water can be sculpted into all kinds of fanciful shapes. Here are the basic options:

■ A short, heavy, burbling column of water rising vertically from an open inlet pipe below the pool's surface.

■ A burbling column of water from an open inlet pipe above the pool's surface. This column rises higher than one that begins below the surface.

■ A fine, forceful spray coming from an inlet pipe with a spray jet smaller than the pipe's diameter. The spray rises vertically, describes a graceful arc, or rotates—depending upon the fountain head's design.

Popular spray heads include bell, mushroom, and calyx domes, cascade and aerating jets, many multi-tiered patterns, swivel jets, and spray rings with multiple, adjustable jets.

Design and location. The main rule in spray fountain design is this: Use a short, heavy column of water in windy spots. Go for height, distance, or drama only where the spray will not blow widely, drenching spectators and wasting water.

Professional designers try to position a spray fountain against a background that dramatizes the water's movement. Water in a heavy column tends to be translucent, so backgrounds ought to be dark. Fine sprays appear best when outlined against a flat surface. Heavy sprays dominate and stand out even against a lacy bower of leaves.

As water rises higher, the pool diameter must increase proportionately; otherwise, a steady loss occurs as the water falls, especially in a windy gar-

A Fountain Sampler...

Mollusk, bird, fish...no animal is safe from being immortalized in a fountain. The snail fountain at far left is a handsome variation on the spray fountain theme. The splash sculpture's cranes at center launch water skyward, only to get it right back. At right, a dolphin and riders wrestle through the years in a classic splash sculpture.

den. A general rule of thumb is that the basin should be a minimum of twice the diameter of the spray's height.

Unless you're building a bubbler fountain (see page 26), install the jet just above the water level. If your pool will include water plants or fish, plan the installation very carefully. Water lilies don't like heavy turbulence, though fish can benefit from the aeration a remote fountain provides. (For details, see Chapters 4 and 5.)

Hardware and accessories. Your spray fountain requires a submersible or recirculating pump (see page 15) to recycle water, plastic tubing to connect pump and fountain head, and, ideally, a separate drain connection. A control valve allows you to fine-tune fountain output from a soothing trickle to a thundering roar.

You'll also need a 120-volt, GFCI-protected receptacle for the pump, a switch to activate the fountain, and a separate switch for optional fountain lighting. Submerged, movable light fixtures positioned directly below the spray create the most drama; low-voltage halogen downlights are effective for pinpointing special features. Timers and color blenders that are programmed to automatic sequences can also be purchased for submerged light fixtures.

The simplest and most economical method of installing a fountain is to purchase a complete unit at a retail outlet or directly from the manufacturer. No plumbing is required. You simply put the kit together, fill the bowl with water, add an algicide, and connect the fountain unit to an electric power source. Other fountain assemblies include a pump, strainer, valve, and fountain head (and, in some cases, lights), all mounted in a single, compact, submersible base; you pick the pool.

Splash Sculpture

The wide range of designs for splash sculpture fountains suggests a long history. For centuries, pumping water up through a sculpture to splash over a series of surfaces into a pool has been a favored form for fountains. The water inlet was traditionally a Grecian urn or other art object, held by a cherubic nymph or symbolic figure. Nearly every city in Europe has a public square that displays some variation of the splash sculpture fountain style.

Remember, though, that a formal fountain requires lots of room. If you want to place a splash sculpture fountain in a limited space, you can scale down the design. A metal sculpture gives a strong contemporary appearance. Avoid using a traditional stone sculpture in a modern pool; artistic balance is a tricky accomplishment.

You will find both traditional and modern sculptures in stone and metal on sale at garden sup-

...Plus Three

A handcarved Mexican lion head and a tranquil Japanese bamboo spout are at opposite ends of the style spectrum, but they're both examples of spill fountains. The architectural fountain at right shows the effects of elegant lighting on moving water. Landscape architect for the lion fountain: Jeff Stone Associates. Bamboo fountain: landscape ceramist, Cevan Forristt.

DO-IT-YOURSELF
FOUNTAINS

Pleasing fountains and pools can be surprisingly simple. We show three designs here, but your own ingenuity will suggest more.

Installation is easier than ever before, with the ready availability of compact, inexpensive submersible pumps and tough pool liners. Water and energy costs need not add up: a small pump that circulates 140 gallons of water per hour over a 3-foot drop uses less electricity than a 70-watt light bulb, costing about 1/2 cent an hour.

You can convert a wooden planter box, a metal basin, or a large pot into a small fountain. Coat the inside of a wooden container with asphalt emulsion or epoxy paint, or use a flexible liner. If you're using an unglazed pan or clay pot, coat the interior with asphalt emulsion, epoxy, or polyester resin; a dark-colored sealant enhances the water's reflective quality. Then drop in a submersible pump with riser pipe (in shallow water, a few rocks can conceal the pump) and add water.

For larger holding pools, many designers prefer precast rigid fiberglass or reinforced concrete. PVC sheeting is an excellent, if less permanent, water holder; flexible liners can also go beneath concrete for extra water-holding insurance.

Any piece of hardware with a smaller aperture than that of the riser pipe can work as a homemade fountain jet: automotive grease fittings, drip irrigation components, and brass lamp conduit and caps are just three possibilities.

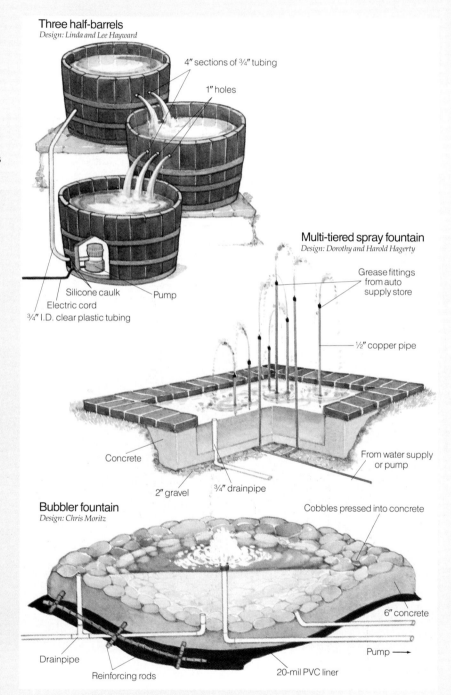

Three half-barrels
Design: Linda and Lee Hayward

4" sections of ¾" tubing
1" holes
Silicone caulk
Pump
Electric cord
¾" I.D. clear plastic tubing

Multi-tiered spray fountain
Design: Dorothy and Harold Hagerty

Grease fittings from auto supply store
½" copper pipe
Concrete
2" gravel
¾" drainpipe
From water supply or pump

Bubbler fountain
Design: Chris Moritz

Cobbles pressed into concrete
6" concrete
Pump →
Drainpipe
Reinforcing rods
20-mil PVC liner

ply centers, stone-cutting yards, and import stores. A few department stores also stock them. You can commission both stone and metal sculptures, usually at the artist's studio or at a gallery acting as the artist's agent.

Spill Fountains

Whether a spill fountain is an ordinary household pipe pouring water into a container, a series of spill pans attached to a wall, or a scaled-down version of the great Roman ornamental fountains, it is nearly always designed to capture a specific characteristic of falling water or create a particular tableau. For some people, the simple sound of falling water is adequate; others may want the fountain to carry a symbolic message in its design. Rarely is an attempt made to disguise the water source or to make the fountain appear to be a waterfall. No fountain head is used at the inlet for a fountain of falling water. Spill fountains, because of their customary design and sheltered location, do not usually present a wind problem.

The simplest spill fountain design, and the least expensive, is a single stream of water pouring into a pool or container. The pool can be large or small, depending on the space and budget allotted to it. The classic Japanese *tsukubai*—a hollowed-out bamboo rod trickling into a concave stone basin—is the model of simplicity. To save water, add a small sub-

The Dominant Theme

This garden provides a lavish example of a simple tenet: Use a strong central element to give order and focus to a design. Here, the star-shaped pool that frames the splash fountain dictates the shape of the lawn, flower beds, and paving. Landscape architect: Emmet L. Wemple & Associates.

Courtyard Retreat

Handmade raku wall tiles add the finishing touch to this brick wall fountain, which provides a musical refuge from neighborhood noise and views. The core structure is concrete block; spill shelves are supported by reinforcing rods. A submersible pump recycles the water; a 3-way valve regulates flow and allows drainage. Landscape designer: Michael Glassman/Environmental Creations.

Triple Header

Today's spas are increasingly serving as decorative pools and fountains in the off hours. In this case, three decorative water outlets fill the spa; PVC water supply pipe is directly behind each. Complementary tile colors link the fountain to the spa and surrounding paving. Landscape designer: Mark Gennaro/Landshape, Inc.

mersible pump in a concealed location; a tiny bit of overflow can feed a bog garden surrounding the pool.

Spill pans are available in two- and three-tiered plastic or metal sets that you can purchase at hardware or department stores and garden supply centers. If you have the necessary skills, you can make your own spill fountain from boiler ends or build a series of spill pans from your own materials and design.

More Ambitious: Wall Fountains

Wall fountains were practical public water sources long before the invention of indoor plumbing. The ancient form is seen frequently in Europe, most often along the Mediterranean coast. Water passing through a sculptured figure standing in a wall niche was usually employed to fill a servant's water jar.

Today, the fountain's principal role is ornamental. Water can pour directly into the pool from the pipe, overflow from a basin, or flow directly from a series of spill pans or trays. An increasingly popular variation adds a natural touch to today's swimming pools and spas. Water issues from lions' and gargoyles' mouths, wall niches, spill shelves, or gleaming high-tech nozzles into spa or pool—sometimes via a chain of streams or waterfall-joined holding pools. Indeed, it's hard to distinguish between this type of fountain and an architectural waterfall (see

Chapter 3). The distinction is unimportant; in either case, the effect is delightful.

Building a formal or classic wall fountain is relatively expensive. Not only is the formal fountain itself an extensive project but also the surrounding area must have complementary features if the fountain is to fit into its environment. Submersible pumps and water pipes can be combined to add a fountain to an existing wall. Construction is much simpler, though, if plumbing is incorporated into the wall during the building of the fountain. An electrical switch, perhaps located indoors, controls the pump-driven flow; a ball or 3-way valve allows alteration of the flow to match the mood. If you wish to replenish water evaporation automatically, hook up a float valve (page 16) to your water supply line.

The construction of the raised holding pool is critical: concrete or concrete block work well, covered with plaster or faced with brick, tile, or stone above the water level. Concrete fountains require several coats of waterproofing compound. To leakproof a pool, you can also sandwich a flexible liner (see page 12) between layers of brick or stone.

A wall fountain is typically lit from below each cascade or from the sides with submerged, low-voltage spotlights. Uplighting accentuates smooth sheets of water and projects dancing highlights onto the fountain, surrounding walls, and foliage. A dimmer switch (see page 87) helps set the mood.

Lion on the Loose

Brick, hand-painted Portuguese tile, and one very angry lion team up in this colorful wall fountain. The construction is concrete block coated with waterproofing compound, covered with tile on the inside and back walls and stucco elsewhere. A small exterior pump pulls water from the basin and drives it up to the concrete lion's head; a gate valve allows drainage to the street. Landscape architect: Jeff Stone Associates.

Fountain at Center Stage

Night or day, this fountain commands attention. The aerating jet, lit from below by a submersible low-voltage light, is at the head of a rock-bound stream; for another view, see page 43. Architect: The Steinberg Group. Landscape architect: Eldon Beck Associates.

Heat and Light in the Night

This garden fountain plays a dual role as a heated spa: the underwater pool light can be dimmed for a relaxing soak. Low-voltage PAR-36 uplights accent the palm trees; other fixtures splash light on the birds of paradise. Landscape architects: Fry + Stone.

Midnight Swim?

This poolside fountain's two-tiered structure is plastered concrete faced with [...] outside, a row of blue tile inside. Overhanging slate spillways promote smooth cascades. Lighting is by low-voltage uplights recessed into each holding trough and repeated in the surrounding foliage; all fixtures are dimmer controlled. Landscape designer: Michael Glassman/Environmental Creations.

Classic Cherub

Cast iron maiden arches water from a lily pad, accenting this intimate natural pool. Subtle background plantings, Sonoma fieldstone, and flat border stones blending into slate patio paving all help this quiet corner merge with the surroundings. The figure is lit at night by a built-in pool light. Landscape designer: Kathryn Mathewson Associates.

Bamboo Glade

This spill fountain scene was designed to enhance the view from a home office window. An update of the Japanese tsukubai, *this version has drip irrigation tubing inside the bamboo to keep it from rotting out. The rock pocket was fashioned with a pneumatic hammer. A tiny submersible pump sustains the quiet trickle, controlled by a nearby valve. Landscape designer: Michael Glassman/Environmental Creations.*

Purple Power

Smooth, arching lines and bright, bright color distinguish this wall fountain. Stucco over concrete block core provides a soft look, as do the tiled backdrop and trough and the copper splash shelves. The pool edges function as sitting benches or shelves for plant display. Landscape architect: Jeffrey Van Meren.

Mystery of the Pyramids

Wall fountain, spray fountain, splash sculpture, garden spa: which is the right term for this water feature? Take your pick! Aerating jets shoot up out of two decorative wells; the overflow slides in sheets down the slick tile faces. Additional ledges in the tiles slow the flow, creating the novel water patterns. Landscape designer: Rogers Gardens.

WATERFALLS
& STREAMS

Whether the sight
is one of nature's monumental cascades at
Yosemite National Park or a simple mountain stream falling over rustic terraces
toward the sea, nearly everyone stops to
watch a waterfall. The enchantment of
flowing water is so pervasive that people
often travel hundreds of miles to see it.

Inspired by such visits and wishing
to bring a small piece of tranquility home,
we can build naturalistic waterfalls and
streams of varying sizes in our gardens,
indoor-outdoor rooms, atriums—even in
our living rooms.

"Natural" waterfalls and streams aren't
the only option, either. Today's architectural waterfalls—much like wall fountains
in design and effect—are becoming more
popular in residential situations. Streams
unify a waterfall with a nearby garden
pool, tying the two together and lending
a sense of continuity to the landscaping
scheme. Today's swimming pool is also a
scene for waterfalls; they soften the edges
and create a new focus of interest, as well

Designed by Nature?

*When planning a natural-looking
cascade, take a cue from nature. This
poolside waterfall has carefully placed
native stones, varied channels and
drop-offs, both shallow and deep holding pools, and a symphony of sounds.
Landscape designer: Kathryn
Mathewson Associates.*

as a cooling curtain of water on scorching August afternoons. Streams can unite the spa with the pool, or a garden pool with the swimming pool—even serve as a water slide for adventurous swimmers. An existing stream is another option, even a dry streambed built into a native plant environment.

Remember that waterfalls and streams aren't necessarily a waste of water. What appears to be a never-ending, one-way flow is really a small amount of water circulated again and again by a small pump and connecting pipes.

Waterfall Basics

Architectural waterfalls are obviously man-made, tending to geometric shapes that reflect the urban environment. If you're thinking of building one, take a trip to nearby public squares, looking for designs to scale down, and study wall fountains you like. Or visit a landscape architect or designer and ask to see some formal waterfall designs.

Most do-it-yourself waterfall builders prefer to imitate nature, feeling that native waterfalls take the kind of tumble that looks proper in a home garden. Basically, the idea is to separate two or more pools at different heights so that they will appear to have been formed without man's help. (A torrential waterfall with its source mysteriously placed midway up a property line fence is not likely to appear credible.) The upper pool is usually the smallest of the two, just large enough to achieve a bustling flow of water. The inlet pipe enters below the surface or from a niche among border stones.

Wherever native stone plays a dominant part in a garden waterfall, ample space is a fundamental requirement. Boulders fill up space quickly. Some stones—mainly shales and other striable types—can be stacked in ways that look natural. Massive stones, such as the granites so common in western mountains, look far less at home when stacked.

By paying close attention to scale, it is possible to build a bustling small waterfall from a tiny volume of water. You can arrange fist-sized broken stones to appear much larger. Creative imagination can transform dwarf varieties of native plants into their standard-size counterparts.

Closeup on Waterfalls

Small variations in a waterfall's lip can create subtle effects. As shown at top left, the lip's contour creates a corresponding water pattern. "Pinching in" on the sides, as shown at bottom left, will force the water to take some spectacular tumbles. An architectural waterfall, such as the one at right, opens up a whole new realm of possibilities.

A Fall That Feeds Both Spa and Pool

This rock-bound fall—seemingly spilling right out of the house—tumbles down to a heated spa and swimming pool. A 30-mil plastic liner ensures a watertight base, with concrete on top; the cascades are further treated with a waterproofing compound. The framing boulders are secured in mortar, and others are simply stacked. Landscape designer: Michael Glassman/Environmental Creations.

Designing the Falls

How do you lay out a natural-looking waterfall? Carefully observe the way nature builds hers:

■ Stubborn flat rocks fortify the center of the stream, forming the edge of the falls.

■ Water rushes along lines of least resistance—between, around, and over the firmly entrenched stones—washing away dirt, gravel, and all other loose material.

■ Nature frames the falling water's path with stones cast aside or worn away by the rushing water and with appropriate plantings.

Water can take whatever course, direct or circuitous, you choose. You can opt for a more-or-less continuous waterfall—either a single "freefall" or interweaving channels—or for one that breaks into a series of holding pools or stairsteps. Step falls usu-

ally look best when the pump is shut down, as water remains in the small pools.

The placement of rocks is what really makes or breaks your fall's character. Irregular rocks in the center of the channel create a rapids effect. A big boulder at the base froths the water up even more. An overhang of several inches is best for a curtain effect; some designers add an acrylic lip to keep water from dribbling down the rock face (the acrylic is invisible unless viewed up close). Pinching in the sides of the fall compresses the water, forcing it into a thicker curtain. Gaps, grooves, and other irregularities in the lip create unique patterns.

There are no firm rules here. The key is experimentation—moving a rock here, a rock there—until the waterfall looks and sounds its best. What better excuse to kick off one's shoes, roll up one's pantlegs, and become a kid again for a few hours?

Tropical Paradise

Flat stones protrude from outlet slots to shape these clean, refreshing freefalls. The waterfalls are repeated all the way along the back wall of this extended swimming pool, creating the tropical look. The wall is concrete faced with Bouquet Canyon stone. Landscape designer: Mark Gennaro/Landshape, Inc.

Accent Falls

Your waterfall doesn't have to be an imitation of roaring Niagara Falls to be successful. This tiny version graces the hillside in perfect counterpoint to the elegant lamppost. A little concrete, some selected stones, and a small submersible pump are the basic ingredients. Design: Philip Neumann.

Waterfall Nuts & Bolts

The typical starting point for a waterfall project is either a natural incline or the mound of subsoil excavated for a garden pool. The entire face of the falls must be sealed to keep water from escaping and to prevent dirt from washing into the lower pool.

Your options are traditional concrete, premolded fiberglass watercourses and holding pools, and PVC, butyl-rubber, or other pool liners (see page 12). Hide the edges of the channels with natural stones and plantings. For construction details, see pages 78–79.

Water plants cling to remarkably precarious snatches of soil once established. The key is to form "pockets" of protected soil adjacent to or between waterfall channels, sealing the gaps between border stones with mortar. Try to place the mortar on the side away from view. Without mortaring, resign yourself to a certain amount of soil washing into the water with each rain.

You'll need a submersible or recirculating pump (see page 15) to move water from the bottom pool back up to the top, where gravity will send it on its way again.

Waterfalls for easy installation are sold by pump and fountain manufacturers. You can also buy simulated rock that appears almost realistic. Viewed from across a room, these waterfalls may appear very realistic, but such installations do not invite close scrutiny.

Would You Like to Build a Stream?

Streams are as varied as any of nature's other creations. There are rushing streams amid granite mountains, lazy streams in upland meadows, and muddy streams through farm valleys, ranging in size from a tiny trickle to awesome rapids.

Before building a garden stream, a homeowner would be wise to settle on a single design drawn from his or her own experience. Streams designed only from imagination tend to encounter difficulties with nature's laws.

Water moving at a languid pace will wander through curves, always washing the outside bank of the curve. Streams, therefore, tend to grow wide at the midpoint of a curve. They become shallower along the inside because water moves more slowly and silt is deposited along the inside curve.

A fast stream rushes in a straight line, detouring only where rocks bar its path. The rushing water tends to keep such a streambed free of mud.

The choice between a slow- or fast-moving stream depends upon the topography of your land

Man-made Spring

This rock was cracked already and, with a little additional persuasion, was fitted with a water supply pipe and positioned as the perfect "natural source" at the head of this backyard stream. To produce a thicker flow, additional water issues from just below the rock. The handsome plantings reinforce the impression of a mountain spring. Landscape designer: Michael Glassman/Environmental Creations.

BRIDGES &

STEPPING STONES

The simplest way of crossing a small stream is over large stepping stones set in the water. This is not really a bridge but an extension of a path. Materials include poured concrete shapes, sliced log rounds, quarried flat stones, and natural boulders. For greater visual interest, lay stepping stones at an angle to the banks or stagger them. Close spacings are safer and induce visitors to linger awhile.

For wide streams and pools, you'll probably need a bridge instead. The design should plan for a bridge 2 to 3 feet wide to promote a sense of security for those who walk across it; a railing is recommended for long bridges or those over deep water.

Three basic bridge building materials are wood, cast concrete, and quarried stone. Wood is the commonest, most versatile, lightest, and least expensive. Three basic designs are shown below. Arched or flat, straight designs are the norm, but a zig-zagging bridge (called *yatsuhashi* in Japan) encourages a leisurely stroll.

You can cast a slab bridge in reinforced concrete right on the spot. Pour the concrete into a pre-built form, and when it has set remove the sides of the form but leave the bottom—it'll never be seen.

Quarried stone is a frequently used bridge material in Japanese-style gardens, but it's tricky to work with for beginners. Some garden supply centers or specialty stone yards may have curved granite slabs that will give an arch to a stone bridge. Since these are imported from Japan, they are much more expensive than either a wooden plank bridge or one you cast yourself.

For spanning a distance of more than 4 or 5 feet, a bridge structure should be supported by a foundation, or by midspan piers or posts. A foundation can be merely two blocks of concrete, one at each end, poured directly into holes dug in the ground. Set a couple of reinforcing rods vertically into each foundation before you pour, letting them extend far enough that you can secure the bridge structure to them. When the bridge is in place, conceal the foundation with soil, rocks, and plantings.

Piers can be made from pressure-treated poles or 6 by 6 posts sunk into the bottom of a pond or wide stream to give center support to a bridge. Simpler yet, support the center of a low bridge on a large rock.

Flat, unarched bridges should be 6 inches to a foot above the surface of the water; if the distance is much more than that, the feeling of intimacy may be lost. To further tie bridge and water together, arrange stones both on the banks and in the water beneath the end of a bridge.

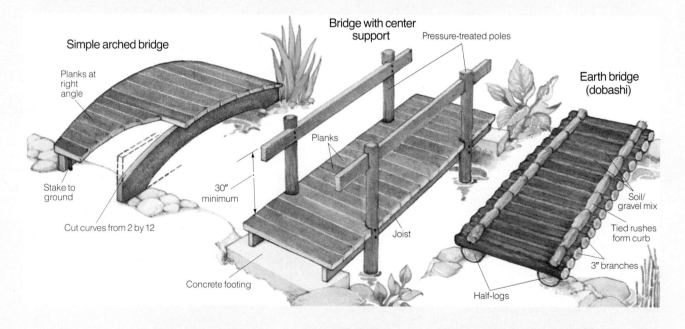

Simple arched bridge

Planks at right angle

Stake to ground

Cut curves from 2 by 12

Bridge with center support

Pressure-treated poles

Planks

30" minimum

Concrete footing

Joist

Earth bridge (dobashi)

Soil/ gravel mix

Tied rushes form curb

3" branches

Half-logs

and may be entirely governed by the landscaping requirements of your site.

In a private garden, a "natural" stream ought to provide the kind of flow that your property can handle easily. Unless your stream burbles mysteriously out of the ground, the rushing water usually has a waterfall as its source. In this case, the water must be pumped from where the stream ends (perhaps where it flows into a pool) back to the waterfall, where it begins its journey again. An architectural stream typically issues from either a spray jet or a wall-mounted inlet.

Although a contemporary stream might be walled with angular brick, stone, stucco, or adobe, the typical natural stream is hand-packed concrete, overlaid with natural stones or pea gravel. Loose-aggregate concrete also creates a pebble-like effect. Streams may be fashioned from flexible liners (with or without concrete on top) or premolded fiberglass sections: camouflage edges with stones, turf, or border plantings.

Though we think of a natural stream as flowing noticeably downhill, most garden streams work best if laid out level or at a very gentle pitch. To negotiate a steeper slope, lower each level section as a unit, connecting sections with small cascades or falls. To create turbulence, decrease the depth of the channel slightly, narrow the banks, or add stones. Always build a deeper channel than you think you'll need: seasonal runoff can flood low banks. Alternately, plan an overflow course of perforated plastic drain pipe to a well-drained spot.

Working with an Existing Stream

If you are fortunate enough to have an existing stream running across your property, you've already saved construction time and expense. But if you want to change the stream in any way, be sure to contact the Department of Fish and Game in your state. Laws govern all stream changes, and the laws are very strictly enforced. In most areas, you will also need to contact your county and municipal planning officials.

In redesigning and changing the bed or course of a stream, take great care to keep each changed factor in scale with the rest of the stream bed. Oversights can be disastrous. Note where currents will work against soft banks and the extent of scouring action; in time the stream may chart a third course, to your great distress. Damming a stream to start a waterfall may bring the water level to a point at which it can exert force against a weak spot if left unguarded.

Multiple Choice

Is it a fountain? A stream? A waterfall? An architectural statement? It's all of the above. Water issues from a copper spout (fashioned by a sheet metal shop) cemented into the architectural column. The water then flows along the concrete block and plaster stream trough and plunges down the tile-lined falls (see inset below). A recirculating pump picks up the water and sends it back to the spout. Landscape architects: Jeff Stone Associates and Lois Sherr.

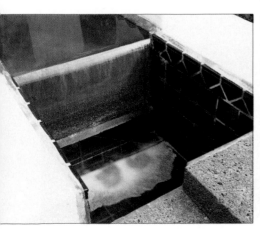

Wettest Way Down

Whooooaaa! This stream doubles as a water slide; his slippery route to the pool curves through ferns and horsetails and between boulders. The slide is steel covered with plaster and troweled to a glass-slick surface. Landscape architect: Ned Bosworth.

Spa-to-Pool Creek

In this scene, a short, splashing accent stream links the spa and the nearby pool. Matching stonework on the spa steps, streambed, and pool lip ties the units together; border plantings emphasize the natural look. Landscape contractor: Grimes Natural Landscape, Inc.

Spaside Niche

A poolside spa provides a sheltered niche for this architectural waterfall. Handsome stonework, held together with mortar, sets the scene. The fall, designed like a wall fountain, has multiple outlets—above, below, right, and left— and a pair of rock-hewn spill shelves to create a variety of special effects. Landscape designer: Rogers Gardens.

Flagstone Terrace

After a number of meandering turns and spills, this flagstone-lined stream finds its way to a collecting pool near the bottom of the terraced courtyard. At night, each cascade is illuminated by a portable, sealed light fixture—one is visible in the stream channel at center. Architect: The Steinberg Group. Landscape architect: Eldon Beck Associates.

Cascading Tropical Stream

From its beginnings on the sheltered hillside, this stream makes its way through two upper pools, bends around a corner, and plunges between tight banks to a third holding pool. The basic structure is gunite shot over welded wire mesh; the large rocks were positioned before the pour, then smaller rocks and gravel were patted into the wet concrete to create the "riffle" effects. Landscape architect: Todd Fry.

Granite Falls

Water wells up into this koi pond over a granite-lipped waterfall; notches in the sloped lip funnel the water into graceful sheets. Pond consultant: Paul Cowley/ Potomac Waterworks.

A Cooler for Cats

A freeform concrete stream is one of the simplest types to make; a flexible liner makes it watertight. Border plantings, rocks, and a small footbridge soften the concrete edges.

High-country Cascade

Sonoma fieldstone boulders, dams and niches, colorful flowers, and ground covers team up to make this poolside waterfall a natural delight. The inspiration was a cascade in Yosemite's high country. When a waterfall is designed, only experimentation will show which configuration of rocks and channels creates just the right water volume, sights, and sounds. Landscape designer: Kathryn Mathewson Associates.

WATER
GARDENS

Gardening possibilities multiply instantly when you add a pool to the landscape. In contrast to their long-accustomed, frequent problem of providing adequate drainage for plants, pool owners face an entirely different form of gardening in which plants often thrive in water alone.

From water lilies to floating, oxygenating, marginal, and bog plants, your choice of water plants is wide and varied. On pages 48–51, we take a look at the general characteristics and uses of each category, then offer planting suggestions for various garden situations—deep water, marginal shallows, and surrounding bog gardens. For illustrations and descriptions of specific water plants, see pages 52–55.

Which plants are sure-fire winners in your microclimate? It's a good idea to ask the local nursery personnel or another pool owner in the neighborhood; or call a mail-order supplier that sells a selection of plants nationwide (mail-order listings are on page 95).

Drifting Colors

The surface of your garden pool affords a shimmering "canvas" for Impressionist gardening arts. Shown here are tropical water lilies 'Blue Beauty', 'Dauben', 'Golden West', and 'Margaret Mary'. Lilypons Water Gardens, Lilypons, Maryland.

Floating Plants

Floating water plants break down into two basic types: (1) Those with their roots in the soil and their leaves floating on the surface—water lilies, for example; and (2) Floating plants such as water hyacinth or water lettuce, whose roots simply dangle in the water.

Rooted plants, sometimes called "semi-floaters," not only are beautiful, but help keep the pool healthy by providing shade and crowding out competing algae. They don't like heavy turbulence, so plant them away from the splash of a waterfall or fountain.

True floaters grow and multiply with great speed, gobbling up open water. Water hyacinth grew so rapidly when introduced in Florida streams that the plants became a menace to navigation. On the other hand, water hyacinth is considered an excellent purifier, soaking up ammonia and other potential toxins. Keep floaters away from koi, for the fish shred the roots, which in turn clog the pump.

Oxygenating Plants

These hard workers grow submerged beneath the pool's surface. Although they do not bloom and are rarely seen, they are, nevertheless, indispensable to a balanced water garden. Oxygenators such as Anacharis are frequently employed in indoor fish aquariums; they take up carbon dioxide and release oxygen to other plants and fish. In fact, you can often see tiny oxygen bubbles clinging to the surfaces of these plants. Oxygenators also provide a spawning area for fish and a handy hiding place for small-fry until they get big enough to fend for themselves.

Maintaining Margins
Colorful marginal plants help define your garden pool environment. Water irises, shown at left, are a natural with natural pools; so is the Japanese maple in the background. Above, umbrella palms soften the formal shapes. By planting in containers, you can move the plants as your moods—and the seasons—dictate. Filoli Gardens, Woodside, California.

Marginal Plants

Some water plants do best around the pool's margins, with their heads waving in the breeze and their feet in shallow water. Two classic examples are the Japanese iris and the umbrella plant. Most marginal plants prefer water 2 to 6 inches deep. These are the plants that benefit from a separate, adjoining shallow area in your pool or a series of shelves around the edges. Marginal plants help provide a smooth transition from pool to border in both formal and natural garden pools.

Bog Plants

Some plants grow best around the pool's borders where water splashes, keeping the ground wet. These bog plants camouflage the concrete or fiberglass edges of a pool, waterfall, or stream, lending a natural appearance. They can also extend the "water" environment, making the pool look larger or tying it to the surroundings. These plants often come from families seen in the garden at large—for example, primrose, lobelia, and calla lilies.

Two worthy mentions, not really bog plants but often associated with natural pool settings, are bamboo (many varieties are available) and Japanese maple (*Acer palmatum*).

Planting Techniques

Here's the number one rule for planning your water garden: Plant with restraint. Consider the mature growth of the plants when figuring layout and spacing; be sure to plant large marginal and bog plants well back from the edges of the pool. A garden sketch is a big help.

The Tall & Short of It

Above, horsetails form a tall, linear backdrop to this tranquil scene off the master bedroom. The adjacent floating plants are water four-leaf clover and parrot's feather. Design: Bill and Caroline Furnas. At right, thick layer of water lilies 'Marliac Carnea' and 'William Falconer' carpets the foreground; towering above is the pink lotus 'Roseum Plenum'.

ALL COLORS IN THE RAINBOW—

THE WATER LILIES

Water lilies (*Nymphaea*) will almost certainly be more widely planted when more gardeners begin to appreciate their beauty, their dependability, and the ease with which they can be grown. Lilies come in both hardy and tropical varieties. Hardy water lilies bloom during daylight, opening about 10 a.m. and closing after sunset, but tropicals include both day and night-blooming versions.

Hardy types are the easiest for a beginner to grow and can overwinter in the pool. Tropicals—larger, more prolific bloomers, available in a greater selection of varieties and colors—must be considered annuals in all but the balmiest climates. With some effort, however, they can be rescued and stored carefully in a greenhouse or other cozy spot.

Plant hardy water lilies from early spring through October in mild-winter areas. Although the tropicals can be grown in all areas, they shouldn't be planted until average daytime temperatures rise above 65 degrees—normally after the first of May. If set out at the recommended times, water lilies begin to flower in 1 to 4 weeks. Hardy lilies flower early in April and tropicals produce their first blooms in May.

The best tropicals will bear up to three times as many flowers as the hardy lilies. Most flowers live 4 days, once open; they last just as long if they're cut. (To keep cut flowers open, apply melted paraffin or candle wax with an eyedropper around the base of the stamens, petals, and sepals.)

You can grow all kinds of water lilies in a pool with vertical sides and a uniform depth of 18 to 24 inches. If the sides of the pool have a gradual slope, the water there is subject to extreme temperature variations that are unhealthy for your water plants. And, algae grows faster in the shallows.

Both hardy and tropical water lilies require full sun—4 to 6 hours each day is minimum—to open the flowers. If you have to build your pool in partial shade, choose a location that gets the morning sun.

Use a heavy garden soil for planting water lilies but don't add manure, peat moss, or ground bark to the soil. Manure encourages the growth of algae and fouls the water, and peat moss and bark will float to the surface and cloud the water.

Mix about a pound of slow-acting, granular-type fertilizer with the soil for each lily that you're planting. A complete fertilizer with a nitrogen content between 3 and 5 percent is considered almost ideal. Most water lily growers sell a specially formulated fertilizer.

Plant only one water lily in each container so that the leaf pattern of each plant will be displayed to best advantage. Cover the soil with about an inch or more of pebbles to prevent clouding the water. The top of each container should be 8 to 12 inches below the surface of the water.

Tropical lily 'Yellow Dazzler'

Tropical lily 'Attraction'

To further avoid the "jungle" look, arrange your plantings so they'll form the kind of progression or backdrop you'd like (for example, delicate plants up front; taller, leafier species in the back). Plan the layout to take advantage of different color schemes and seasons. For example, water hawthorn blooms in winter and provides a punch of color when water lilies die back.

Choosing containers. In pools less than 2 feet deep, it is possible to plant directly into soil at the bottom of the pool. Most water gardeners, however, like the versatility of movable containers that allow easy access to the plants, which facilitates pool cleaning and allows better plant control. Floating plants don't really need rooting, but a container will help isolate and contain these invasive plantings. Small containers also help control the spread of oxygenators.

One way to go is to use wooden crates, wire mesh baskets, or pulp containers, all lined with burlap, but simple plastic tubs and buckets—from 5 to 32 quarts—are inexpensive, easy to obtain, and won't decompose into a gooey mess in the water.

Basic planting procedure. Plant your water plants in a pocket of heavy soil, but don't worry too much about its content; the plants take most of their nutrition from the water. Leave about an inch at the top of the container, then cover the soil with pebbles or fine gravel to prevent clouding the water and to discourage rooting fish.

Some water plants have specific depth requirements (see pages 52–55); simply adjust the height of their containers with bricks or concrete blocks (be careful not to tear a pool liner). Some water plants need to be closer to the surface when young; then they can be lowered to their more permanent depth when established. Simply build them up on bricks or blocks and gradually remove the blocks as the plants become established.

Water lilies and some other water plants are not at all fond of heavy turbulence, so be sure to locate them out of the direct splash zone of a fountain or waterfall.

Marginal plantings. A narrow shelf built into the pool makes it easy to arrange your marginal plantings; it needn't go all the way around the perimeter. Add shelves when pouring a concrete pool, or dig them out before installing a liner. Fiberglass pools are often sold with integral shelves. For details, see Chapter 6, "Building Your Pool."

Another option is to partition off a "pocket" area for plants, using a stone or brick dam. Adding this feature, or building a formally divided pool, will keep koi from the water plants if you want the best of both worlds.

Creating a bog garden. Normally, gardeners need to fight for adequate drainage of plants. In a bog garden, you try to retain water. The splash from the pool will do for many plants; or you can simply lay a pot in the water with its lip above the surface or backfill the pocket area (see "Marginal plantings," above) with heavy soil and gravel. More formal bog gardens can be designed by running an overflow pipe from the pool and/or by using a liner below the garden to retain water. For specifics, see page 77.

Planting Profile

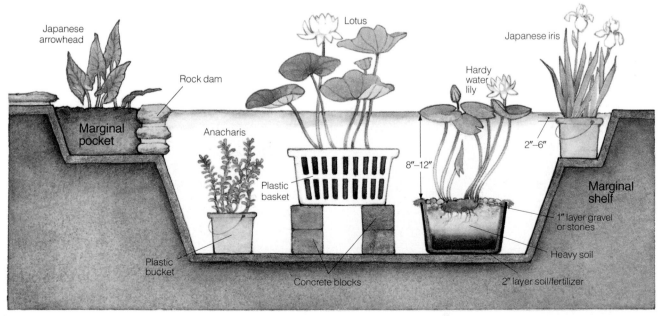

Japanese arrowhead · Lotus · Japanese iris · Rock dam · Marginal pocket · Anacharis · Hardy water lily · Plastic basket · 8"–12" · 2"–6" · Marginal shelf · Plastic bucket · Concrete blocks · 1" layer gravel or stones · Heavy soil · 2" layer soil/fertilizer

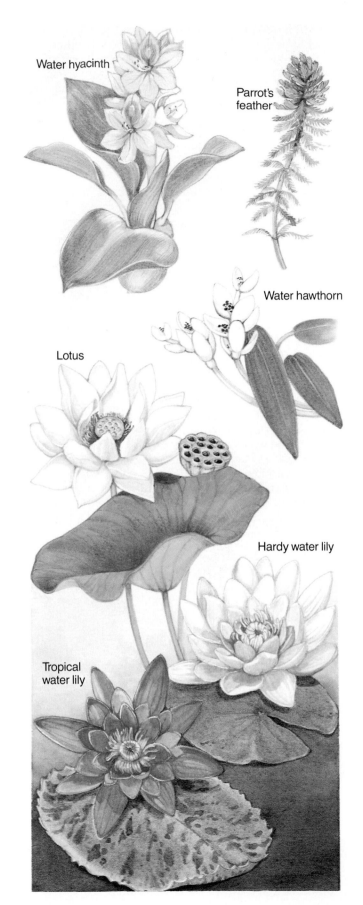

Water hyacinth

Parrot's feather

Water hawthorn

Lotus

Hardy water lily

Tropical water lily

A Guide to Plant Selection

Scores of plants are available for planting in and around your pool. Below, we describe 34 of the most popular, broken down by basic type: floating, oxygenating, marginal, and bog or border. All of these plantings, and more, can be ordered by mail (see page 95 for listings); many can be found at nurseries in your area. If you're industrious, you might also come across some of these in the wild.

Floating plants. Most of these are actually rooted below the water's surface, with leaves and flowers floating above. True "floaters" simply dangle leaves and roots in the water, although even these fast-growing plants benefit from container planting to keep them under control.

▪ *Floating heart (Nymphoides peltata).* Fuzzy, five-petaled, 1-inch yellow flowers grow atop heart-shaped 2– 4-inch leaves. Spreads by runners, may need cutting back during growing season. Plant in 4–12 inches of water.

▪ *Lotus (Nelumbo).* Available as started plants or as roots; place 8–12 inches below water surface. Thick stems rise from rootstocks in spring, supporting the magnificent round leaves up to 5 or 6 feet above the water surface. Flowers, up to 10 inches across, are held above the leaves and are single or double in pink, white, and pale yellow. Ornamental seed pod, good for dried arrangements, is perforated with holes in salt-shaker effect. Goes dormant in winter; protect roots from freezing.

▪ *Parrot's feather (Myriophyllum).* Has light green, whorled, feathery leaves that drift on the surface of the water. Roots provide a good spawning area for fish. Available at pet stores; plant in 3–12 inches of water.

▪ *Pennywort (Hydrocotyle vulgaris).* Emerald-green, cupped leaves, up to 2 inches in diameter, creep across pool border or float on the water; tiny white flowers rise above. Plant in bog conditions or in shallow water.

▪ *Water four-leaf clover (Marsilea).* Leaves are emerald green, up to 3 inches across, patterned with brown and yellow. Floats on surface forming carpet. Grow in 3 inches or more of water, thin as necessary.

▪ *Water hawthorn (Aponogeton distachyus).* Like a miniature water lily, it produces floating leaves from submerged tuber. Leaves are long and narrow; 1/3-inch-long, white, fragrant flowers stand above water in two-branched clusters. Has a winter flowering habit in mild climates that is unique among common aquatics. Submerge 8 inches below surface.

▪ *Water hyacinth (Eichhornia).* Floating leaves and feathery roots. Leaves 1/2–5 inches wide, nearly circular in shape; leaf stems inflated. Blooms showy, lilac blue, about 2 inches long. Upper petals with yellow spot in center, in many-flowered spikes. Do not turn loose in natural or large bodies of water. Needs warmth to flower profusely.

■ *Water lettuce (Pistia stratiotes).* Also known as shell flower, but does look like floating lettuce. Floats on the water surface trailing its hairlike roots. Although it does fairly well in partial shade, needs daily exposure to the sun. Seems to thrive near a spray of some kind, perhaps a fountain.

■ *Water lilies (Nymphaea).* Leaves float and are rounded, with deep notch at one side where leaf stalk is attached. Showy flowers either float on surface or stand above it on stiff stalks.

Hardy types are easiest for beginner to grow, come in white, yellow, copper, pink, and red. Need full sun in order to bloom. Top of soil should be 8–12 inches below water. Go dormant in fall, reappearing in spring.

For tropical lilies, add blue and purple to hardy colors; recent introductions include yellows and an unusual greenish blue. Some tropicals in the white-pink-red color range are night bloomers; all others close at night. Tropical kinds go dormant but do not survive really low winter temperatures.

■ *Water poppy (Hydrocleys nymphoides).* Has 3-petaled, lemon-yellow flowers, 2 inches across, resembling the California poppy. Flowers and 1–3-inch leaves make thick carpet just above water surface. This plant is attractive if controlled, a nuisance otherwise. Blooms best in 1–3 inches of water.

■ *Water snowflake (Nymphoides indica).* Same genus as floating heart, page 52. White flowers, 3/4 inch wide, feathery like snowflakes. Flowers and heart-shaped leaves float on surface. Plant in 3–12 inches of water.

Oxygenating plants. Oxygenators promote better water quality, serve as fish food, and provide protected niches for fish to hide and spawn in.

■ *Anacharis (Elodea canadensis).* Common aquarium oxygenator, available at pet stores. A perennial, it propagates by runners. Full, slender foliage grows under water. To control it, pinch off the old growth. Anacharis needs a lot of sun.

■ *Duckweed (Lemna minor).* Has tiny leaves that cover a pool quickly. Unless given almost constant attention, this plant can be quite a nuisance. One expert notes that fish eat its tender roots which act as a laxative and serve nicely as a fish tonic.

■ *Eel grass (Vallisneria americana).* Leaves grow long and ribbonlike, as high as 2 feet. A very good oxygenating plant. Submerge 6–24 inches below surface.

■ *Sagittaria (Sagittaria graminea).* Belongs to the same genus as an arrowhead that is planted around the pool, but this one is quite different. Primarily an oxygenator, it grows freely in water with its grasslike leaves mainly submerged.

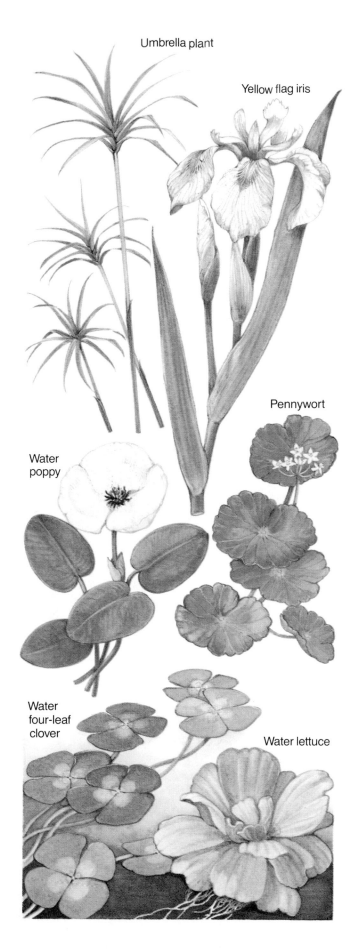

Umbrella plant

Yellow flag iris

Pennywort

Water poppy

Water four-leaf clover

Water lettuce

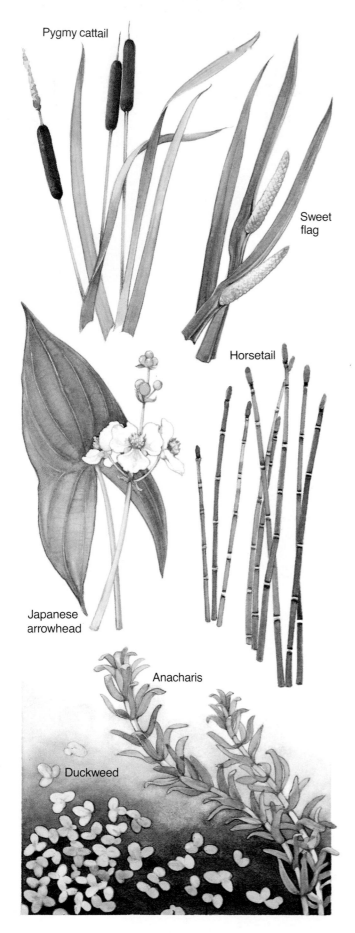

Pygmy cattail

Sweet
flag

Horsetail

Japanese
arrowhead

Anacharis

Duckweed

Marginal plants. These help camouflage pool edges and enlarge the water garden environment. Generally, marginal plants like 2–6 inches of shallow water, but most tolerate more or less.

■ *Chinese water chestnut (Eleocharis dulcis).* Dense, rushlike, cylindrical stems rise 1–3 feet; tubers at base are a well-known ingredient in Asian cooking. Grow in up to 12 inches of water.

■ *Horsetail (Equisetum hyemale).* One of the most popular pool plants, this vigorous grower is best controlled in a container, whether planted in or near the pool. Slender, hollow, 4-foot stems are bright green with black and ash-colored ring at each joint. Spores are borne in conelike spikes at end of stem. Effective in sunny or partially shaded garden situations.

■ *Papyrus (Cyperus papyrus).* Known as Egyptian paper plant. Tall, graceful, dark green stems 6 to 10 feet high, topped with clusters of green threadlike parts to 1-1/2 feet long. Will grow quickly in 2 inches of water in shallow pool, or can be potted and placed on bricks or blocks in deeper water. Protect from strong wind.

■ *Pickerel weed (Pontederia cordata).* Gives wild-pond look to informal garden pool. Roots grow below water, long-stalked leaves stand well above water; these are heart shaped, to 10 inches long and 6 inches wide. Short spikes of bright blue flowers top 4-foot (or shorter) stems. Can be sunk in up to 12 inches of water.

■ *Pygmy cattail (Typha minima).* This species is a smaller version of the common cattail, more in scale with small pools. Two feet tall and slender with familiar brown pokers on top. Plant in up to 12 inches of water. Invasive.

■ *Umbrella plant (Cyperus alternifolius).* Narrow, firm, spreading leaves arranged like ribs of umbrella at tops of 2– 4-foot stems. Flowers in dry, greenish brown clusters. Grows in and out of water. Good accent plant, can become weedy and take over a small pool.

■ *Water canna (Thalia dealbata).* Grows 3–4 feet tall, with spear-shaped 6–9-inch bluish green leaves and spikes of purple flowers. Will grow in mud or several inches of water. A few true Canna hybrids perform similarly, but most should be restricted to poolside.

■ *Water iris (Iridaceae).* Several species of iris thrive in pools or at poolside. All have narrow, swordlike leaves and showy flowers. Japanese iris (*I. ensata, I. kaempferi*), grows to 4 feet, bears 4–12-inch flowers—white, pink, blue, and purple—in early summer. *Iris laevigata,* also native to Japan, has smaller flowers in blue or blue and white, and thrives in shallow water, as does 5-foot Yellow flag (*I. pseudacorus*). Siberian iris (*I. sibirica*) with blue, purple, or white flowers, likes drier soil, grows 1–2-1/2 feet high.

Bog/border plantings. Normally, these are used for borders or in a formal bog garden; however, many are quite at home in shallow water as well.

■ *Arrowhead (Sagittaria latifolia).* From dark green, arrow-shaped leaves emerge spikelike clusters of 1-1/2-inch white flowers. Grows to 4 feet tall, in bog conditions or submerged up to 6 inches deep. Thin occasionally.

■ *Baby's tears (Soleirolia soleirolii).* Creeping, moss-like, perennial herb with tiny white flowers makes cool, luxuriant ground cover near pools. Use it where it won't be stepped on, in shade.

■ *Bog arum (Calla palustris).* Waterside plant, good for hiding edges of small pool. Grows 10–12 inches high, spreads laterally. Leaves 6 inches long, arrow shaped; flowers green outside, white inside. Red berries succeed flowers.

■ *Bog lily (Crinum americanum).* White, droopy, 4–5-inch flowers grow on stalks up to 2 feet tall; very fragrant. Leaves are long and slender. Plant in up to 6 inches of water.

■ *Candelabra primrose (Primula japonica).* Hardy Candelabra has stout stems to 2-1/2 feet with up to 5 whorls of purple flowers with yellow eyes. Blooms May to July. Likes semi-shade, lots of water.

■ *Cardinal flower (Lobelia cardinalis).* Erect, single-stemmed, 2–4-foot-high plant with saw-edged leaves set directly on the stems. Spikes of flame red, inch-long flowers. Summer bloom. Sun or part shade. Border planting in moist soil or in water up to 2 inches.

■ *Elephant's ear/Taro (Colocasia esculenta).* Tropical elephant's ear has mammoth, heart-shaped, gray-green leaves; stalks fast-growing to 6 feet. Thrives in warm filtered shade with protection from wind; plant in moist soil or in up to 12 inches of water. Hawaiian staple food poi is made from the starchy roots. Violet-stemmed taro is a smaller variety.

■ *Marsh marigold (Caltha palustris).* Bog plant up to 2 feet tall, well adapted to edges of pools, streams. Sun or shade. Green leaves 2–7 inches across; vivid yellow flowers are 2 inches across, in clusters. Lush, glossy foliage gives an almost tropical effect.

■ *Plantain lily (Hosta plantaginea).* Has scented white flowers, 4–5 inches long, on 2-foot stems. Leaves bright green, to 10 inches long. Many similar types of Hosta. A good poolside planting.

■ *Sweet flag (Acorus calamus).* Fans of grasslike leaves resemble miniature iris; 1/4-inch-wide leaves, 1-1/2 feet tall. Variation *variegatus* has alternating green and cream-colored stripes. Plant at pool edge or in shallow water.

■ *Weeping sedge (Carex pendula).* Subtle, grasslike clumps soften a pool's edge; long, narrow, evergreen leaves, drooping spikes. One of many species of sedges appropriate for water gardens.

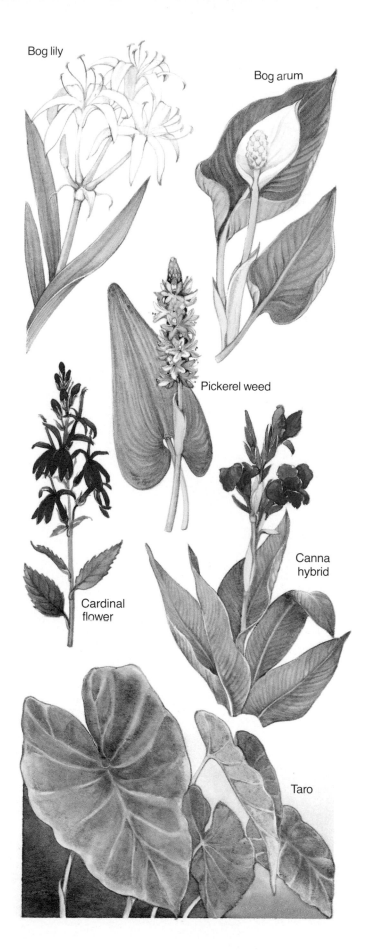

Bog lily

Bog arum

Pickerel weed

Cardinal flower

Canna hybrid

Taro

GOLDFISH
& KOI

What's a garden pool without a lazily swimming school of goldfish or koi, softly gleaming in the sun? With some basic care, fish can be quite comfortable in your garden. On the following pages, we'll present the basics of fish-raising; for help in selecting your goldfish or koi, see the drawings and descriptions on pages 62–63.

For many of us, goldfish invoke memories of small, sloshing fishbowls lugged home as prizes from county fairs; contrary to our best intentions, the fish often died very soon. Why? As you'll learn, goldfish need plenty of oxygen and well-balanced water; the classic fishbowl is one of the worst possible designs in both of these regards.

Japanese koi become family pets, coming when called, following owners around the pool, taking food from outstretched fingers, even allowing themselves to be petted. These creatures outlive almost any other kind of pet, and they may even outlive their owners.

All Dressed Up

As shown at left, koi carp present a kaleidoscope of colors and patterns. These are just youngsters; in coming years they could grow as long as 2-1/2 feet. Golden State Fisheries, Sacramento, California.

Pond Fish: An Introduction

Goldfish, koi, and numerous other pond fish are available for stocking your garden pool. Here's a rundown of each basic type.

Goldfish. These perennial pets come to mind automatically at the mention of fish ponds in a garden. Goldfish have been bred for centuries as hobby fish; consequently there are countless types, and they are a good choice for a small pool. They're normally quite docile and can be mixed among themselves and with other types of fish; don't expect them to be as outgoing and friendly as koi.

Common varieties for outdoor ponds include Common, Comet, Calico, Fantail, Moor, Shubunkin, and Veiltail. More exotic species include the Lionhead, the Oranda, and the exceedingly strange Celestial. For details on these types, see page 62.

The Golden Orfe and Green Tench are two scavenger fish for hobbyists; both are European imports. Scavengers can help reduce algae and pond wastes. The Green Tench hides out at the pool bottom; its more gregarious cousin, the Golden Orfe, spends much more time at the surface.

Young goldfish haven't yet developed their distinctive colorings and are much less expensive than their larger kin. Just make sure they're 2 to 3 inches long when you purchase them; smaller fish have a great fatality rate. In an outdoor pond, some varieties of goldfish may reach lengths up to 10 or 12 inches. Under friendly conditions, you can expect your goldfish to live about 3 to 4 years; 6 to 12 years is considered a very long life.

Koi. Japanese koi, or *nishikigoi*, aren't goldfish; they're colorful carp. How can you tell the two apart? Koi have two pairs of whiskers, called *barbels*, on their upper mouths; goldfish do not. Breeders name them for their colors; they're bred to be viewed from the top. There are single-color, two-color, three-color, and multi-color varieties. A German variety of armored koi has been interbred with Japanese types to produce *Doitsu*, which are either armored or "scaleless" varieties. For details on koi types and nomenclature, see page 63.

A Wild Pond—Right Off the Deck
Pickerel weed, water lilies, and swirling fish make a wild statement here. The owners can observe the proceedings from the very civilized deck.

The Nitrogen Cycle

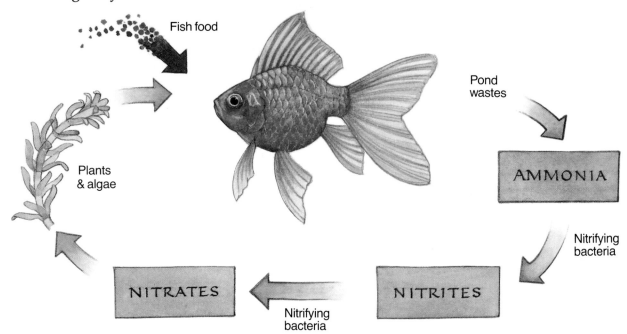

Fish food

Plants & algae

Pond wastes

AMMONIA

Nitrifying bacteria

NITRATES

NITRITES

Nitrifying bacteria

Koi grow much bigger than goldfish: lengths of 27 inches or even 3 feet are not out of the question. With thoughtful care, a koi's potential life span is up to 60 years; one Japanese koi reputedly lived for over 200 years.

Prize koi specimens command great prices. It's best for the beginner to start with inexpensive fish (about 10 dollars), then move up as you become more involved. A koi club or helpful dealer can help you start off on the right track.

Other pond fish. Additional fish choices break down into small types, such as minnows, guppies, and tropical fish; and larger game fish, normally stocked in lakes and streams.

Generally, very small fish are unsuitable for ponds. They certainly can't compete if mixed with koi or goldfish (they may be gobbled up by their bigger poolmates). Tropical fish simply can't take the typical temperature fluctuations. A few minnows or other small-fry, however, help keep a tub garden free of insects and algae.

Game fish such as catfish, bluegills, and crappies are available for large ponds, but you'd best check with the Department of Fish and Game—they're banned in some areas. Many game fish have very specific temperature and aeration requirements, making them unsuitable for backyard pond life. These species may attack other fish.

Balancing the Water

Fish need oxygen just like land-based creatures; they absorb it from water passing through their gills. To ensure that they'll get enough air, the pond's surface area must be as great as possible; in addition, some aeration—in the form of a fountain or waterfall—is beneficial. A small air pump, designed for the purpose, can provide extra aeration in still ponds and keep beneficial bacteria alive if the main pump fails.

A bigger problem is ammonia in the water. Fish respiration and other wastes produce ammonia; additional sources are uneaten food and plant debris on the pool bottom. The key to understanding ammonia build-up—and its eradication—lies in the nitrogen cycle (see drawing above). In the presence of beneficial bacteria, ammonia is reduced to nitrites, which in turn break down into nitrates, which can be taken up by plants and fish. Biological filtration is one way to deal with ammonia; mechanical filtration with zeolite as the medium is also touted by some experts. Natural filtration from plants such as the water hyacinth can be very effective, but you'll need to change the plants every 30 to 60 days. To monitor the ammonia situation in your pool, buy an ammonia test kit. Ponds with detectable levels should be treated with partial water changes or with a product intended for this purpose.

Other water problems include chlorine and chloramines. Chlorine, which is added to most municipal water supplies, is bad for fish in large amounts; fortunately, it will dissipate in a few days if left standing. Chloramines (combinations of chlorine and ammonia) are very toxic; and as more and more water suppliers are adding these to tap water, you'll have to take chemical steps to break them down.

POND

PROTECTION

Once you've established your fish pond, you may find that your friends and neighbors aren't the only ones interested in the progress of your goldfish or koi. Domestic explorers like the family cat or neighborhood basset hound, or wilder visitors such as herons, raccoons, and even skunks, may drop by looking for a little fun or the proverbial free lunch. Any one of these can devastate a prized fish collection in a very short time.

How do you ward them off? Sufficient pond depth, 24 inches or deeper, is a big help. Most mammals can't latch onto your fish while swimming; they must find solid footing in the pool. Overhanging pool borders and dense marginal plants provide fish with a temporary hiding place; so do hollowed-out "islands" made from wood or stones and covered with water plants. A pond running underneath a deck, with a solid wall above water and fish-sized openings below, is another option. Netting is the surest solution for marauding herons, though this is usually the least satisfactory option esthetically.

An electric fence wire, anchored to insulated posts and strung completely around the pond area, is very effective if carefully installed; these low-voltage units are available from hardware stores and some garden pool catalogs. At the high-tech end of the spectrum, you can install a motion-sensitive alarm, but be prepared for false alarms.

The pH (acidity) levels are also important. Whenever you're filling up a new pool, let it sit for a couple of weeks before introducing the fish. Concrete pools must be cured; check the pH of the water with a pH testing kit. The best pH for a fish pond is between 6.8 and 7.6.

Proprietary products for getting your pool water in shape are available from pet stores and mail-order sources. Don't make frequent water changes in your fish pond—not only is it a waste of water, but you'll need to treat it for chlorine, chloramines, and pH constantly. Instead, top up with a little bit of fresh water as necessary.

For more details on balancing and maintaining your pond water, see "Maintaining Your Pool" on pages 90–95.

Designing the Fish Pond

A fish pond can be any shape. However, adequate depth for koi is crucial. It must be no shallower than 18 inches and ideally between 24 and 36 inches, or deeper. The pond must also be large enough so the fish have room to swim. Figure on 1000 gallons as the minimum for a koi pond; that translates to a pool roughly 10 feet long by 8 feet wide by 20 inches deep. (To calculate pool volumes, see the feature box on page 91.) Goldfish can survive in smaller spaces.

If your pool is for fish only, place it where it gets some shade. This is good for the fish (colors tend to be richer and deeper in shade) and will keep down algae formation.

Surface exchange of oxygen and other gases is important, so don't cover more than 50 percent of the surface with floating plants. Protect new plants in cages until well established, and add rocks atop soil in plant containers to keep fish from rooting. A separate marginal area for plants, protected by a rock dam—or even better, a divided pool—is best for pool owners devoted to both plants and fish.

Goldfish live comfortably in water ranging from 50 to 80 degrees but prefer the narrower range from 60 to 70 degrees. Koi don't mind a change in water temperature if it's gradual. There's less temperature fluctuation in deeper pools.

If you really want to enjoy your colorful fish, pool water should be as clear as possible. Pool filters will keep the water clear; the best fish ponds often have a combination of biological and mechanical filter—typically, a pressurized-sand filter. The constantly operating biological filter is the workhorse; the pressure-sand unit simply serves as a "polishing" filter. But we've seen pools with no filters that are crystal clear. Water is simply well balanced or circulated so that fouled water is forced up a pipe from the bottom. For plumbing details, see Chapter 6, "Building Your Pool."

Introducing Fish to the Pond

One rule of thumb for stocking goldfish or koi in your pond is roughly 1 to 2 inches of fish for every square foot of surface area. But a better formula is *patience*. Simply start off with a few fish and work your way up. If your fish are healthy, your filtering system is in top shape, and the water is well aerated, you can add new fish to your collection.

Most fish arrive in a plastic bag containing a small amount of water and a blast of pure oxygen. When transferring your fish to the pool, float the bag on the surface for at least 15 minutes, which lets the water temperature in the bag gradually adjust to that in the pool. (If the day is warm and sunny, shade the bag with a towel.) Next, open the bag and let the pool water enter, then ease the fish into the pool. They'll probably take off and hide; gradually, over a period of days, they should begin to feed.

If you're introducing new fish into an established pond, many experts recommend that you place them in a quarantine pool, or separate tank, for up to 3 weeks. This will enable you to screen the fish for unusual actions or diseases; if a fish is sick, it can be treated before the entire pond is infected.

Feeding

The number one rule to remember is this: Don't overfeed your fish. They can only eat a small amount at a time and the rest sinks to the bottom where it quickly fouls the water. Feed them the amount they can eat in five minutes; no more. If they're hungry, fish nibble at insects in the pool and on algae or fast-growing oxygenating plants.

Goldfish and koi are omnivorous: they'll eat almost anything. Packaged fish foods, containing a balance of protein, carbohydrates, and vitamins, are recommended; some koi foods include spirulina (a high-protein algae) or carotene as "color enhancers." Floating foods won't foul the water; uneaten pellets can easily be netted and removed from the pond. Diversity is healthy for fish. Basic rations can be supplemented with table scraps and live foods; pet stores carry worms, daphnia, brine shrimp, and ant eggs for special treats.

As winter approaches and the water temperature dips, fish appetites decrease. At about 45 degrees, koi begin to effectively hibernate, living off body fat until spring and warmer water rouse them from dormancy.

Dinner on the Veranda

Koi are the prized tenants of this front-yard fish pond, which is complete with a state-of-the-art filter system. At top, koi dine from their built-in feeding shelf. A rock dam, shown at right, keeps the fish from munching the water plants for dessert. Landscape designer: Dennis Tromburg/Zierden Landscaping.

Veiltail

Chinese
Black
Moor

Japanese
Fantail

Shubunkin

Comet

Lionhead

A Guide to Goldfish

Goldfish have clearly discernible types, varied in color, fin size and shape, body shape, and even eyes. They also come with an assortment of scale patterns: matt (without luster), nacreous (mottled), and metallic. Here's a description for each type you're likely to run across.

■ *Common.* The "original model" from which the fancy varieties were developed. Has short fins all around, is an excellent swimmer, and is very hardy. Though color is normally orange gold, sometimes has other markings: silvery types are called *Pearl;* yellow types are called *Canaries.* Black patches often change to red with age.

■ *Comet.* Similar to the Common, but the body is a "stretch" version, with larger fins all around and a much longer and more deeply forked tail. The fastest of the fancy goldfish varieties, the Comet does very well in outdoor pools.

■ *Shubunkin.* Resembles the Common goldfish in shape, but *London* or *Calico* type has matt scales, beautiful colors—pale-blue background flecked with red, blue, black. The *Bristol* Shubunkin has larger fins.

■ *Fantail.* Double tail and fins, heavy egg-shaped body. Swims with deliberate, leisurely pace. Two popular types are the *Calico* (scaleless, colors like the Shubunkin) and *Japanese* (goldfish coloring). Fins and tail much longer than Common, drape down; body is rounded. Fins and tail should not be ragged.

■ *Veiltail.* Fins and tail are even longer than Fantail's, drape down; body is rounded. Fins and tail should not be ragged. Most popular type is *Calico.* The *Telescope* Veiltail has protruding eyes, poor eyesight.

■ *Chinese Black Moor.* Velvety black, body small and chunky, profile shape similar to Fantail, telescoping eyes. The only truly black goldfish.

■ *Lionhead.* Sought-after fish with short, chunky body; typically has gold or red-and-white coloring, but some are dark. Claim to fame is "raspberry-like" head growth, which increases with age. Has no dorsal fin, which makes it a poor swimmer.

■ *Oranda.* Similar to Lionhead but has a dorsal fin, which makes it a better swimmer. Not as much head growth. Good specimens shaped more like a Veiltail.

■ *Celestial.* A truly bizarre-looking fish; pupils are on top of the eyeballs, looking *heavenward,* hence the name. The Celestial and its close cousin, the *Bubble-eye,* are risky choices for a fish pond, as they can't see well enough to swim or feed competitively.

■ *Golden Orfe.* A European introduction new to the U. S.; technically a scavenger but comes to the surface to feed. Elongated body, up to 12 inches long, gold coloring. Fast swimmer, quite gregarious.

Japanese Koi Varieties

Japanese koi carp are differentiated by color, pattern, and scale type. Basically, fish can be divided into single-color, two-color, three-color, and multi-color categories. Scales may be *muji* (matt) or *ohgon* (metallic); in addition, *Doitsu*, German types, can be either heavily scaled or "armored," or scaleless ("leather skin"). Pattern distinctions include *Matsuba* (pinecone pattern), *Bekko* (tortoise shell), and even eye color.

If there is a koi club in your area, you might join it. More knowledgeable members will help you in your purchases and recommend the best dealers. Koi clubs also sponsor shows where you can learn which fish are considered the best in their class.

Some of the more popular koi varieties, listed in order from single to multi-colored, are as follows:

- *Shiromuji.* One-color, white with flat scales.
- *Kigoi.* One-color, yellow with flat scales.
- *Akamuji.* One-color, flat red.
- *Ohgon.* Metallic gold or orange gold in color; one of the most popular koi types in North America.
- *Shiro Ohgon.* Platinum metallic, popular variety. *Gin Matsuba* is metallic silver with pinecone pattern as well.
- *Kohaku.* Red on a white background. This group, with many sub-categories, is extremely popular; most champion koi are Kohaku type. The exact patterns determine type—Inazuma Kohaku, for example, has "lightning" pattern; Nidan Kohaku has two red patches.
- *Bekko.* Two-color koi with a tortoise shell pattern. *Shiro Bekko* is black-on-white, *Ki Bekko* black-on-yellow; *Aka Bekko* black-on-red.
- *Utsuri.* Two-color koi types: *Shiro Utsuri* is black-and-white, *Ki Utsuri* black-and-yellow, and *Hi Utsuri* black-and-red.
- *Asagi.* Light blue on top (dorsal) part of body, some red on head and below. May have pinecone pattern, have normal scales, or be armored (Doitsu) type.
- *Shusui.* Similar to the Asagi in color, but always has Doitsu scales. Head and back are light blue, with red below. Prominent dark blue scales run down the middle of the back.
- *Taisho Sanke.* Popular three-color koi variety. Taisho Sanke has red and black markings on a white background. A variation, the *Tancho Sanke,* is predominantly white with one red spot—or "rising sun"—on the head only, and small black patches behind.
- *Showa Sanke.* Similar to Taisho Sanke, but predominantly black with red-and-white markings.
- *Goshiki.* There are many multi-colored koi, but the goshiki is the most prized. It has five discernible colors: red, white, black, blue, and brown.

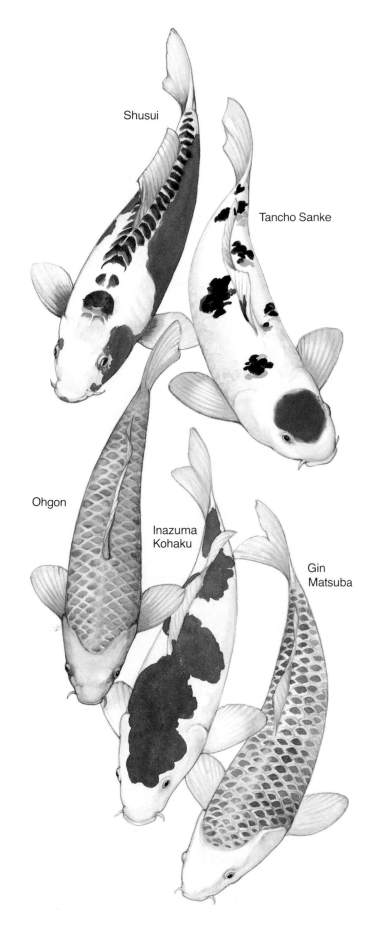

Shusui

Tancho Sanke

Ohgon

Inazuma Kohaku

Gin Matsuba

BUILDING YOUR POOL

In the first five chapters, we focused on general pool planning guidelines, materials, and case studies in color photos and captions. Now it's time to show you how to build your garden pool, fountain, or waterfall.

This chapter covers construction methods for four basic pool types: flexible pool liners; rigid fiberglass shells; poured concrete pools; and concrete block pools veneered with stone, brick, or ceramic tile. Later sections tackle the ins and outs of pool plumbing, plus electrical wiring and outdoor lighting. In the final section, we present guidelines for maintaining your pool through the seasons.

Always check local ordinances and building codes before embarking on a pool-building project: restrictions may include pool site and surroundings, concrete construction and reinforcing, plumbing materials and installation, and electrical wiring. If you're in any doubt about design or your own abilities, a landscape architect, designer, or contractor can provide the help you need.

Pool in Progress

A flexible liner follows the contours of any hole you dig; here, the pool is being filled slowly to stretch the liner into shape. Masonry or another edging treatment will hide and protect liner edges. For more details, see pages 66–68.

INSTALLING A FLEXIBLE LINER

What's new in constructing garden pools? For do-it-yourselfers, it's flexible plastic or butyl-rubber pool liners. By applying a bit of elbow grease, even a beginner can fashion an average-size lined pool in a weekend's time. (Plantings and borders will take somewhat longer.) Here's a step-by-step account of the process.

Planning the size and shape. Before ordering the liner, create a design and figure the finished length, width, and depth of your pool. Remember, simple shapes usually look the best. Once you've come up with a design you like, add twice the pool's depth to its width, then tack on an extra two feet; repeat this procedure to find the correct length. In other words:

Liner size = $2d + w + 2$ ft. by $2d + l + 2$ ft.

For example, a pool roughly 5 feet wide by 8 feet long by 2 feet deep would require a liner 11 feet by 14 feet or the next larger size available.

What if you want an unusual shape? This is no problem, because the rectangular liner can handle a number of curves and undulations. Also, you can weld two pieces of liner together—or have the manufacturer or supplier do it for you.

Marking the layout. Take a garden hose or a length of rope and trace the intended outline of your pool, allowing about 2 inches extra all around for a layer of sand. Stand back and take a look from all sides—and from above if you have a second-story or veranda view. Once you have the perfect outline, pound in stakes to mark the corners or hold the hose in place while you're digging.

Making the excavation. Now it's calorie-burning time. Dig around the outline first, using a good sharp spade. If you're cutting into a lawn, peel back and remove the sod and keep it in a shady spot (you may need it for patching around the border).

Flexible Liner, Step-by-Step

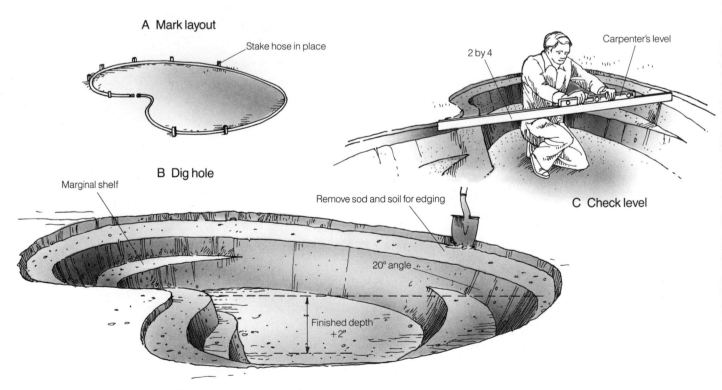

A Mark layout

Stake hose in place

2 by 4

Carpenter's level

B Dig hole

C Check level

Marginal shelf

Remove sod and soil for edging

20° angle

Finished depth + 2"

To lay a solid foundation for your liner, first mark its outline with a hose or a length of rope (A). Excavate the hole, adding 2 inches all around for a layer of sand (B). Check the level carefully with a carpenter's level, using a straight board to bridge the rim (C).

To prepare a brick or flagstone edging (see page 76), remove the sod from that area, too, and dig down just the thickness of the edging material. You may also wish to lay out a bog garden at this time.

The ideal angle for pool sides is about 20 degrees, which will prevent them from caving in and will help keep the liner snug. Do you want to add marginal shelves? The normal dimensions for plant shelves are about 10 inches deep and 10 inches wide, but varied shelves—for boulders and other landscaping—lend the pool a more naturalistic look. You won't need to figure extra liner for shelves.

When you begin to dig, add an extra 2 inches to the depth for a bed of sand. Keep measuring the depth as you go, or mark it on a stake and use that to chart your progress.

A large pool requires a lot of digging, especially if it's deep and the soil is hard-packed or rocky. A small backhoe, sometimes available with a driver, can make life easier.

Leveling the top. Water seeks its own level, so any discrepancy in the height of your pool's rim will be highly visible. Not only is it unattractive to see exposed liner, it's asking for trouble from abrasion and ultraviolet (UV) light degradation.

The simplest way to check the level is with a long, straight 2 by 4 and a carpenter's level. For a small pool, simply bridge the hole with the board; for a longer span, drive a center stake and use it as a pivot to measure out to all sides.

What if the pool is out of level? You'll need to rework the high side or build up the low side slightly. Shaving the high side is best, as loose, unsettled fill can't stand up to much water pressure.

This is the time to rough-in any plumbing or wiring, such as a drain line, a GFCI, or a lighting circuit. For details, see pages 80–89.

Adding sand. To protect the liner, remove all rough edges—roots, rocks, and debris—from the excava-

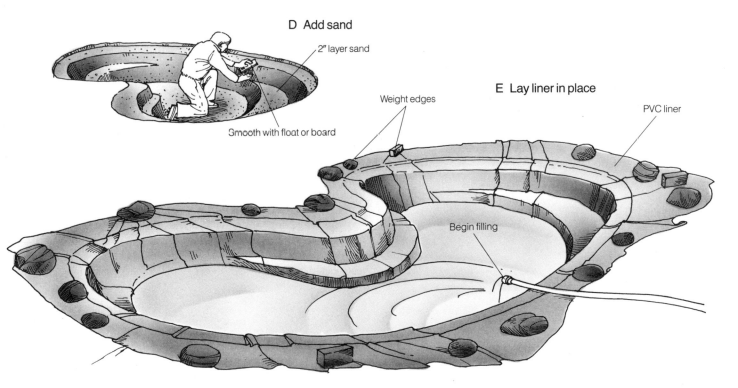

D Add sand

2" layer sand

Smooth with float or board

Weight edges

E Lay liner in place

PVC liner

Begin filling

Next, remove all protruding roots and rocks, fill the holes, and pack a 2-inch layer of clean, damp sand into the excavation (D). Smooth the sand, then drape the liner over the hole, evening up the overlap all around. Slowly begin filling the liner with water (E).

tion, fill any holes, and tamp down soft soil. Lay a 2-inch layer of fine, damp sand over all surfaces (your supplier can help you figure the amount). Spread the sand evenly, packing it into place, and smooth the surface with a board or a concrete float.

Positioning the liner. Warm up the liner by stretching it out in the sun. If you need to make a seam, now's the time. Use the solvent cement and method recommended by the maker of your liner.

Next, with a helper, center the liner over the excavation, draping the excess over the sides. Temporarily weight down the edges with bricks or stones; then slowly begin filling the pool. After adding 2 inches or so of water, start smoothing the liner into shape; sharp corners may require a folded pleat or two (you won't see the pleats once the pool is filled). One brave soul will probably need to roll up his or her pantlegs, wade in, and tuck the liner into place as necessary. The water's weight will make the liner fit the contour of the excavated hole. Continue working, adding a few inches of water at a time, until the pool is full.

Trimming the excess. Now make your way around the perimeter of the pool, adding a little soil here and there to level the top. Trim off the excess liner, leaving about 6 inches to tuck under the edging. For more security, push some long spikes through the edges into the subsoil below. Save the liner scraps for future repairs.

Finishing up. Your pool is ready for the border treatment. Flagstones or bricks laid in a thin bed of mortar are two popular choices—for instructions, see page 76. Native stones, a rock garden, and a bog garden are other options.

Drain the pool to rid it of any impurities from the building process. If you've installed a drain, this is easy; if not, either siphon the water off to lower ground with a hose or use a submersible pump or sump pump to push the water out.

Then fill the pool with fresh water and it's all set for the finishing touches. If you're adding a water garden or fish, first see the water-preparation tips on page 91.

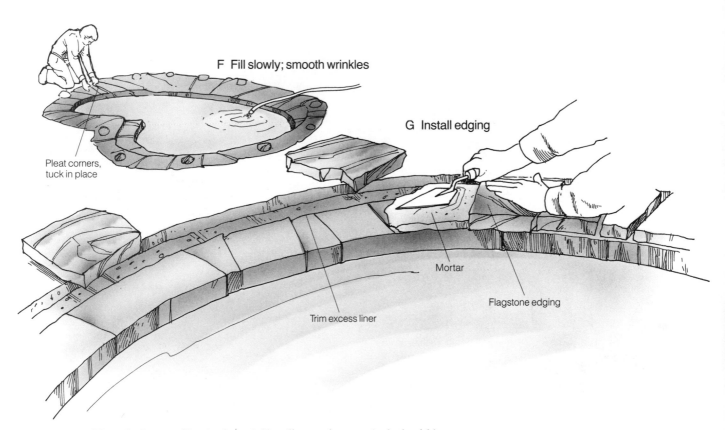

Continue filling the liner, tucking in the wrinkles all around; as required, also fold pleats at hard corners (F), tucking them into place (the water will mask the folds). Finally, trim the excess liner all around and install the edging of your choice (G).

A POOL BUILDER'S

CHECKLIST

This chapter treats each part of the spectrum of pool-building operations—from installing a flexible liner to wiring outdoor light fixtures—as an individual subject. But below, we've devised a checklist to show you at a glance what's involved in building all four basic pool types: flexible liner, fiberglass shell, poured concrete, and concrete block with veneer. The lists will give you a feel for the interrelated tasks involved, as well as help you chart your progress. Before you start work, though, be sure to bone up on the specifics elsewhere in the chapter.

Flexible liner *(see pages 66–68)*

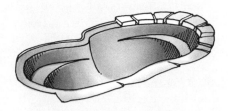

1 Choose site
2 Excavate for pool, marginal shelves, and edging
3 Dig trenches for drain and water supply lines (if any)
4 Dig trenches for wiring (if any)
5 Install GFCI receptacle for pump (if any)
6 Rough-in plumbing and wiring (if any)

7 Pack excavation with 2 inches of sand
8 Position liner; weight edges
9 Begin filling with water; tuck in folds
10 Trim excess liner
11 Apply edgings and borders as required
12 Drain and refill pool
13 Treat water as required

Fiberglass shell *(see pages 70–71)*

1 Choose site
2 Excavate hole
3 Dig trenches for drain and water supply lines (if any)
4 Dig trenches for wiring (if any)
5 Install GFCI receptacle for pump (if any)
6 Rough-in plumbing and wiring (if any)

7 Pack hole bottom with 2 inches of sand
8 Position shell
9 Backfill and add water in 4" increments
10 Add edgings and borders as required
11 Drain pool; refill
12 Treat water as required

Poured concrete *(see pages 72–73)*

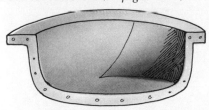

1 Choose site
2 Excavate hole
3 Dig trenches for drain and water supply lines (if any)
4 Dig trenches for wiring (if any)
5 Rough-in plumbing and wiring (if any)
6 Line excavation with gravel

7 Add steel reinforcement
8 Pour concrete
9 Waterproof or paint concrete
10 Finish plumbing and wiring
11 Add edgings and borders as desired
12 Cure concrete
13 Fill pool; treat water as required

Concrete block pool *(see page 74)*

1 Choose site
2 Excavate footings and pool floor
3 Dig trenches for drain and water supply lines (if any)
4 Dig trenches for wiring (if any)
5 Rough-in plumbing and wiring (if any)
6 Form and pour concrete footings
7 Build concrete block walls

8 Waterproof walls
9 Pour concrete floor
10 Add veneer and/or waterproofing to walls and floor
11 Finish plumbing and wiring
12 Add edgings and borders as desired
13 Cure concrete
14 Fill pool; treat water as required

INSTALLING A FIBERGLASS SHELL

Fiberglass shells are the easiest garden pools to install; and unlike those made with flexible liners, they can be used for semi-raised pools or on sloping sites. The only question mark is whether or not you'll find the shape you want or the right dimensions for plants or fish. The keys to success are maintaining level and providing solid support for the relatively weak fiberglass.

Do you have the perfect shell and location? If so, you're ready to begin the installation.

Marking the spot. First of all, bring the pool into the area and situate it in the correct position. Outline the pool's top edge on the ground with a hose or a length of rope, then add 2 inches all around. (The 2 inches are necessary for the sand you'll add, plus some room for "fudging.") It helps to drive stakes around the outline to keep it in place. Remove the shell and place it nearby.

Digging the hole. If you're working on grass, carefully peel back and remove the sod from the area within the outline and set it aside in a shady place. Dig the outline of the pool with a sharp spade; if you plan a sunken flagstone, brick, or stone border, remove the sod and soil to this width and depth as well. A sizable excavation can be pretty heavy going in clay or rocky soil, so you may wish to hire some help and/or a small backhoe to rough out the area.

Make sure the excavation follows the same general taper as the shell walls, which will take some careful measuring and digging. If your pool includes a marginal shelf, shape this too, again leaving 2 inches extra all around. Take particular care with the depth and shape of the hole's bottom.

If your pool will be semi-raised or on a sloping site, you'll need to install fill and/or a masonry retaining wall in advance. Be sure the fill behind the wall is well-tamped and follows the basic shell shape as described above.

Checking for level. After the hole is roughed out, check the bottom with a carpenter's level. If it's level, you're ready to move on; if it's not, keep dig-

Fiberglass Shell, Step-by-Step

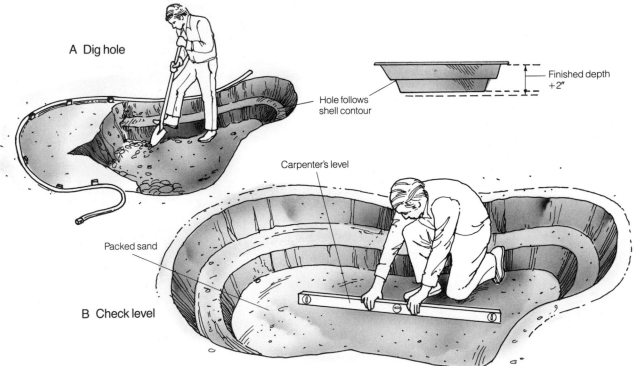

A   Dig hole

Hole follows
shell contour

Finished depth
+2"

Carpenter's level

Packed sand

B   Check level

A properly shaped hole is the key to installing a fiberglass shell: add two inches all the way around, matching the taper and contours of your shell (A). Pack and smooth 2 inches of sand into the bottom, then check it carefully for level (B).

ging and filling until it is. Also remove any sharp objects such as rocks or roots, filling any gaps where these have been removed.

Planning on adding a drain or other plumbing? If so, now's the time for drilling the shell and roughing-in the pipes. See pages 80–85 for details. If electrical wiring is on your list, see pages 86–89.

Adding sand. A 2-inch layer of clean, damp sand comes next; the sand not only helps protect the fiberglass but also supports the shell snugly in its oversize hole. Spread sand evenly only along the bottom at this point, smoothing it carefully and checking again for level.

Positioning the shell. After recruiting some helpers, carefully lower the shell into the hole, and check the top edge for level. If it's off only slightly, you may be able to wiggle the shell into adjustment. If not, promptly remove the shell and level the bottom properly. (You don't want to have to do this after the shell is packed in place and filled with water!)

Backfilling with sand and soil. The secret to success here is patience. Slowly begin to fill the shell with water, and, at the same time, backfill along the sides with mixed sand and soil to support it at all points. Add 4 inches of sand and soil, then add 4 inches of water and check the shell for level. Add another 4 inches of mix, followed by another addition of water and check level. Keep it up until the water reaches the top.

Finishing the job. If you're planning a border around your fiberglass shell, now's the time to install it. Flagstones, fieldstones, and brick all make effective edge treatments. (Pages 76–77 will help with the fine points.) Most owners overhang edgings an inch or two over the water to hide the lip, but some feel the rolled lip looks fine as it is. Seal the joint between the edging and the shell with polyurethane or silicone caulk.

Now finish off any plumbing, treat the water as necessary (see page 91), and your fiberglass garden pool is ready for business.

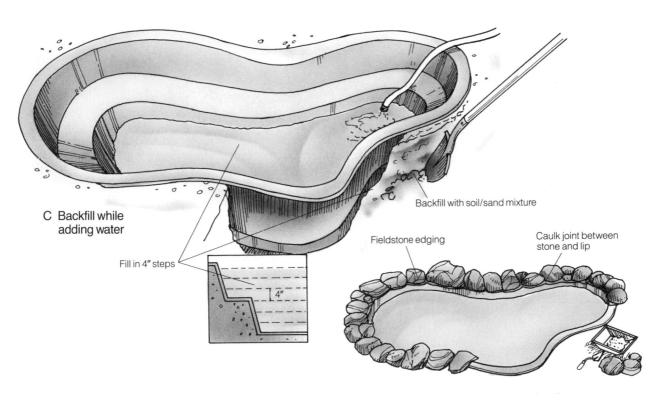

C Backfill while adding water

Backfill with soil/sand mixture

Fill in 4" steps

4"

Fieldstone edging

Caulk joint between stone and lip

D Apply border

Patience is the word now: lower the shell into position, then begin backfilling and adding water in 4-inch increments (C). Once the shell is full, check again for level and install the edging of your choice, overhanging it slightly over the shell edge (D).

THE MATTER OF MASONRY

The great majority of formal garden pools and fountains are still made of concrete, or concrete block in combination with brick, natural stone, or ceramic tile.

Below, we give an overview of the most popular uses of masonry for garden pool construction. Step-by-step instructions are beyond the scope of this book, however. If you need help with your project or you prefer to hire a professional to do the work for you, consult a landscape specialist who installs masonry pools.

Freeform Concrete Pools

A hand-packed concrete pool, such as the one shown on the facing page, is the simplest type of concrete pool for the do-it-yourselfer to build.

First, excavate and compact the pool site. In areas of severe freezing weather, allow an additional 3 to 4 inches for a layer of gravel under the concrete. Walls must be sloped: 45 degrees is about the limit. To prevent runoff from entering the pool in wet weather, allow for a 1- or 2-inch perimeter lip. Marginal shelves of varying widths and depths create a more natural look, and provide solid perches for boulders and other border treatments.

Add reinforcing either by bending 6- by 6-inch welded wire mesh to fit inside the pool or by using 1/4- or 3/8-inch reinforcing rods. Then drive stakes in every square foot, marked either 4 inches (warm climate) or 6 inches (colder areas) above the earth or gravel.

For anything larger than a tiny accent pool, it's a good idea to use premixed concrete—either carted home on a rental trailer or delivered to the site. Ask for "4- or 5-sack concrete with pea gravel," and request it a little on the dry side; the concrete supplier can help you pick the exact mix. For a large pour, you may also need a pump to reach the site from the street.

Using a shovel or trowel, pack the mix firmly around the reinforcing up to the marks on the stakes. Remove the stakes and fill the holes with concrete, then finish the surface with a trowel and cure the shell (see page 75).

To enhance the natural appearance, the walls may be covered with a rock mosaic, set in mortar.

More Advanced: Formwork

Although largely replaced by gunite where fluid shapes are required, and by concrete blocks where they're not, formed concrete is still useful for garden pools requiring crisp, sharp edges. Even a brick or block pool requires a poured floor and footings as a base.

The easiest route to a footing is simply to dig a trench and pour concrete in place in the earth. In cases where the earth is too soft or too damp to hold a vertical edge, you can build a simple form, as shown on the facing page. The footing must be flat on top if a block wall (see page 74) is to be built on top of it.

For the typical semi-raised pool, you can cast the walls at the same time you cast the footings. The combination form illustrated is one example; you can also rent wall forms in some areas. If you're building a sunken pool, you may be able to dispense with wall forms if the soil is firm enough to stand without crumbling. Before pouring the concrete, you may need to add reinforcing rods to both footing and wall forms.

Once the footings and walls have set, lay down 6- by 6-inch welded wire mesh in the floor area and pour a 4-inch concrete slab.

The New Approach: Shotcrete or Gunite

Shotcrete is a mixture of hydrated cement and aggregate applied over and under a reinforcing grid directly against the soil. The mix is shot from a nozzle under pressure, allowing complete freedom of size and shape, since it follows any excavated contour. Shotcrete comes in both "wet-mix" and "dry-mix" versions: the drier mix is called *gunite*.

Because of the specialized equipment involved, however, this is a contractor-only job, but an industrious homeowner can do the excavation and prep work, then call in the contractor for the final application. As part of your prepwork, cover the surrounding area with plastic sheeting or other dropcloths to minimize the effects of overspray.

The basic setup for shotcrete or gunite, as shown on page 74, involves 3/8-inch reinforcing rods, wired together on a 12-inch grid and propped up off the gravel and soil by small rocks. Because the pressure-shot mix tends to "rebound," it's normal practice to add a layer of chicken wire over the gridwork to help secure the mixture. If your pool is on a slope, build up the outside of the shell with sandbags, form the inside, then pull down the sandbags and finish off the outside.

Once the pour is complete, use a trowel to smooth the surface to the desired shape; a rubber glove works well for final smoothing in tough-to-reach areas.

Freeform Concrete Pool

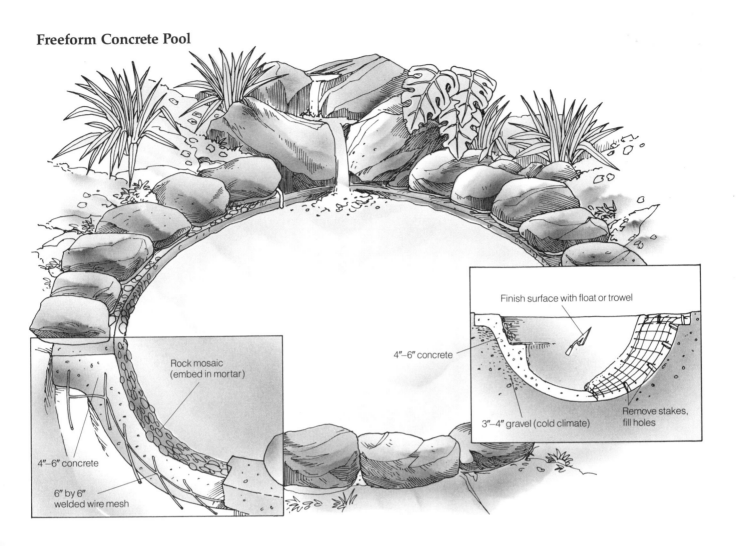

Rock mosaic
(embed in mortar)

4"–6" concrete

6" by 6"
welded wire mesh

Finish surface with float or trowel

4"–6" concrete

3"–4" gravel (cold climate)

Remove stakes,
fill holes

Concrete Formwork

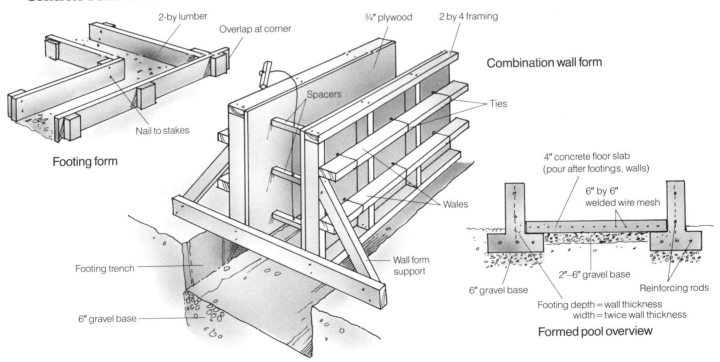

2-by lumber

Overlap at corner

¾" plywood

2 by 4 framing

Combination wall form

Spacers

Ties

Nail to stakes

Wales

Footing form

Footing trench

Wall form
support

4" concrete floor slab
(pour after footings, walls)

6" by 6"
welded wire mesh

6" gravel base

6" gravel base

2"–6" gravel base

Footing depth = wall thickness
width = twice wall thickness

Reinforcing rods

Formed pool overview

Concrete Block

For fast, inexpensive masonry wall construction, it's hard to beat concrete blocks. These rugged units make strong cores for formal pools or wall fountains; for a warmer appearance, veneer them with brick, stone, or tile.

The standard concrete block is a nominal 8 by 8 by 16 inches; actually, each dimension includes a standard 3/8-inch mortar joint. A whole series of fractional units is available to go with it. For veneering, builders often opt for thinner 4- or 6-inch blocks. It's easy to see that with a little planning and care in assembly, you'll never have to cut a block.

The drawing below shows a typical setup for a block-based wall fountain. Bond-beam blocks cap the walls, which, reinforced and grouted, substantially increase the strength. Note also how the corner units overlap for strength. A 4-inch-deep concrete floor completes the structure.

Brick, Stone & Tile Veneers

Veneers are among the most popular applications of masonry. A veneer saves expensive masonry materials by its use only on a project's visible surface, hiding a core of less attractive—and less costly—material.

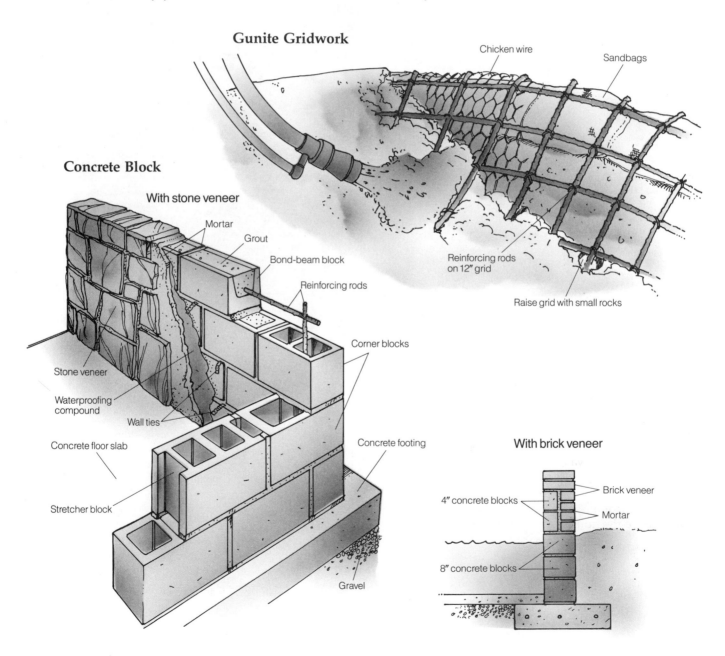

Gunite Gridwork

Chicken wire

Sandbags

Reinforcing rods on 12" grid

Raise grid with small rocks

Concrete Block

With stone veneer

Mortar

Grout

Bond-beam block

Reinforcing rods

Stone veneer

Waterproofing compound

Wall ties

Corner blocks

Concrete floor slab

Concrete footing

Stretcher block

Gravel

With brick veneer

Brick veneer

4" concrete blocks

Mortar

8" concrete blocks

Working with brick. One way to simplify the problems of brick masonry is to make a concrete shell and use it as the watertight interior face. A veneer of bricks on the outer face then produces the desired appearance without needing to be leakproof.

Only a few tools are needed for simple bricklaying: a 10-inch trowel with a pointed blade (for buttering mortar), a brickset (a cold chisel for cutting bricks), a hammer, a 2-foot carpenter's level, a carpenter's square, and a stretch of fishing line.

Brick mortar is a mixture of cement, fine sand, and water, with a small amount of lime or lime putty added for plasticity. Proportions are one part Portland cement, one-half part hydrated lime or lime putty, and four and one-half parts graded sand.

Common bricks should be damp but not wet when they are laid. It is best to build up the corners first and then work at the center section of a wall, using a plumb level to keep the bricks in vertical alignment. Stretch fishing line at each course to keep the horizontal level.

Stone on concrete block. Want to dress up plain concrete block wall? Veneer it with stone. The result appears to be a stone wall, but it can be achieved at much less labor and expense.

When installing a stone veneer wall, you'll need to attach wall ties to the block wall every 2 or 3 square feet. When building the concrete block core, simply insert the ties in the mortar joints between the blocks.

The veneer stones are attached to each other and to the concrete block wall with mortar, the wall ties providing a positive connection to the mortar. Bend as many of the ties as possible into the joints between stones. "Slush fill" the spaces between the wall and the stones completely with soupy—but not runny—mortar as you go.

Dressing up with tile. Poured concrete (especially if roughed-up), concrete block, and brick all make acceptable surfaces for ceramic tile. The tile itself should be a vitreous (nonabsorbent) type for any area in contact with water. In addition, thinset adhesive and grout are recommended, both mixed with latex additive.

Tiling a garden pool is much like tiling the shower inside the house. The basic procedure is this: (1) Prep the surface as necessary for level and plumb; (2) Determine tile spacing and cuts needed; (3) Mark layout lines on the backing; (4) Spread adhesive with a notched trowel; (5) Place the tiles. Once the adhesive is dry (a minimum of 24 hours), spread the grout and sponge it off immediately. Later, polish off the soft haze that sets up.

CONCRETE

TAKES THE CURE

The key to stable, leakproof masonry construction is proper curing, in addition to careful waterproofing or painting.

In concrete lingo, "moist-curing" is the process of keeping the surface wet while it slowly hardens, producing a stronger structure. It's also a good way to rid the new pool of its supply of free lime, which is toxic to plant and fish life. The traditional method is to fill the new pool with water and let it sit for 24 hours. Drain and refill, repeating the process three or four times. The last time, let the water stand for a week and then rinse the pool thoroughly.

In a hurry? Chemical solutions are on the market that get the curing job done more quickly.

Poured concrete pools that will retain their natural color should be given two coats of a commercial, cement-based waterproofing compound. It's best to finish shotcrete or gunite structures with plaster (a professional job), but 3 to 4 coats of waterproofing will also do the trick. Treat concrete block pools with waterproofing compound or another liquid membrane before veneering.

Two kinds of paint can be used on fresh concrete with success, provided the surface is prepared: rubber-base and epoxy. Rubber-base paint should be applied with a brush or roller to a clean surface. Epoxy should be brushed onto a spotless surface. The basic preparatory steps are the same for both types of paint. While the new concrete is still damp (but fully set), etch it with muriatic acid, mixing one part acid to two parts tap water in a nonmetallic bucket. A gallon of muriatic acid will cover from 300 to 500 square feet of surface.

Wearing galoshes, protective goggles (or glasses), and rubber gloves, use a long-handled brush to slosh the acid onto all surfaces. Scrub until the acid ceases to bubble and the concrete attains a uniform, open-grained texture similar to that of fine sandpaper. Wash the acid off and flush it thoroughly out of the pool. (Note: it can cause temporary burns to lawns and plant roots.)

Brush or roll on the paint, usually two or three coats, according to the manufacturer's instructions. Before filling the pool, let the paint dry for 14 days.

EDGINGS & BORDERS

Regardless of the shell material, a good edging (the material directly around the rim) and border (the adjacent landscape) will make or break your pool's appearance. The drawings on these two pages illustrate a number of your edging and border options. Below is additional information on how to work with these materials.

Masonry. In natural pools, masonry is the number one choice for making the transition between water and land.

To lay flagstone or other small stones, first arrange them in a pleasing pattern, cutting stones where necessary with a brickset. Then lay them in 1-inch-thick mortar (three parts sand to one part cement), checking continually for level. Clean the stones with a sponge and water as you work and remove any excess mortar from the perimeter after bedding the stones. Once the mortar has set for 24 hours, pack the joints with the same mix of mortar used for the bed, plus one-half part fire clay to improve workability, and smooth them with a trowel. Keep the grout damp for the first day by sprinkling it repeatedly or by covering it with plastic sheeting,

and keep off the paved area for 3 days to let the mortar harden.

Evenly-spaced bricks are simpler to work with than irregular flagstones. For pointers, see page 75.

Framing a garden pool with large boulders is not an easy way to do the job, but the results can be worth all the toil. Usually these stones look best if partially buried; otherwise, prop them up with smaller rocks, then pack the area with soil and plantings. Here's one trick for placing large rocks: break them with a sledge, move them piece by piece, and reassemble them with cement slurry. Some more back-saving tips: either slide a heavy rock on a large shovel, chain link fencing, or board; or roll it, using a steel bar or plank as a lever.

A mowing strip helps you mow the grass right up to the edge of a formal concrete pool. The strip can either be bricks, set in mortar or packed sand, or a poured concrete strip, screeded flush with simple forms, as shown below.

Wood. In addition to using rock around the edge of a pool, you can use wood posts or logs, in diameters ranging from 2 to 6 inches, to form a series of mini-

Edging Options

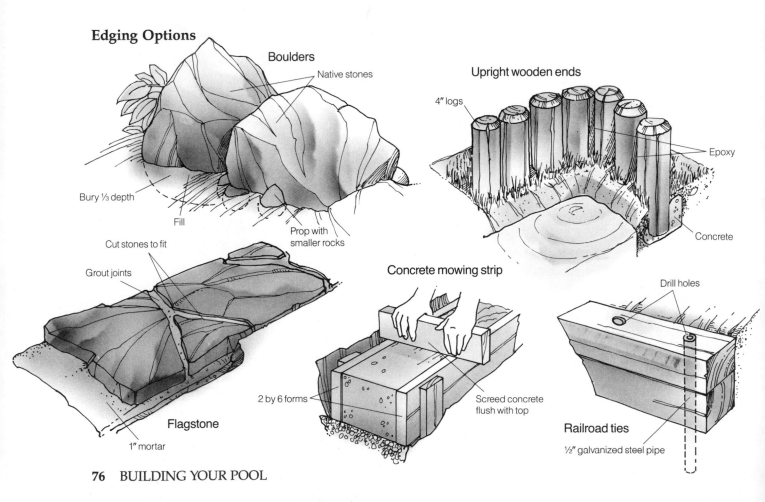

Boulders
Native stones
Bury ⅓ depth
Fill
Prop with smaller rocks

Upright wooden ends
4" logs
Epoxy
Concrete

Cut stones to fit
Grout joints
Flagstone
1" mortar

Concrete mowing strip
2 by 6 forms
Screed concrete flush with top

Railroad ties
Drill holes
½" galvanized steel pipe

ature pilings. Leave the bark on for a more natural appearance. Set the lengths vertically and butted tightly against one another; the bottom ends should rest in concrete, not in bare ground. Add additional concrete behind the pilings.

Railroad ties make effective retaining walls, especially when drilled and threaded with steel pipe, as shown below.

Benderboard forms a curved border for a gravel-edged pool, or serves as a transition between the pool and a surrounding lawn. Wet the boards down before trying to bend them to shape. (You may snap a few boards in the process!)

Running a deck or wooden walkway right up to and over the edge of a pool is another effective trick; make sure any submerged post that supports the deck is pressure treated and rests on a concrete footing and/or precast pier.

Bog gardens, rock gardens. A rock dam, as shown below, is one simple way to accommodate marginal plants. Fill the area with soil, add a short overflow pipe from the pool, and you have a bog garden.

A hillside pool that's shored up on one side presents a good opportunity to construct a rock garden, building up the downhill side with rocks and soil and adding plantings as you wish. If the slope is steep, terrace the rocks, forming crannies for soil where plantings can take a hold. To facilitate watering and to prevent dislodging, set out bank plants in "foxholes" formed by bottomless cans, by circles of aluminum lawn edging, or by buried boxes with the bottoms knocked out. By the time the surrounding material corrodes or rots, the plants will have plunged their roots to a self-supporting depth.

A mound or small berm requires a fair amount of soil, such as that excavated for your pool. Be sure water running off the berm won't enter the pool—a gravel drainage channel or perforated drain pipe (see page 84) is a good solution. Remove any sod and dig the ground up lightly to break the surface crust before you bring in any extra soil for the mound. Then spread out a layer of new soil and, using a shovel or tiller, mix it with the existing soil to ensure good drainage. Tamp it down lightly, smoothing the sides with the back of a rake, and plant the mound as you would any other hillside.

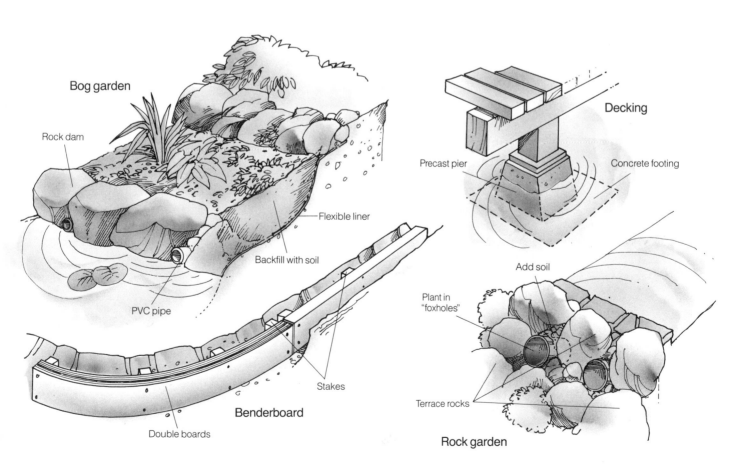

Bog garden

Rock dam

Flexible liner

Backfill with soil

PVC pipe

Benderboard

Double boards

Stakes

Decking

Precast pier

Concrete footing

Add soil

Plant in "foxholes"

Terrace rocks

Rock garden

WATERFALLS & STREAMS

Waterfalls and streams pose some unique technical and design considerations. In the technical department, the number one concern is *waterproofing*. When it comes to esthetics, only creative experimentation will reveal the most pleasing sights and sounds. Both waterfalls and streams benefit from tasteful border plantings.

Waterfalls

Water's continual scouring action plus constant wetting and drying—translated as swelling and contracting—can lead to leaky waterfalls. Therefore, you'll have to take careful steps to ensure a waterproof job. Before plunging into construction, determine the pump, pipes, and other plumbing hardware you'll need (see pages 80–85) to provide the desired flow. Your falls should look good when it's turned off, too.

Selecting waterfall materials. The drawing below shows an overview of one well-made waterfall. The foundation can often be the dirt excavated when you dug your pool, perhaps augmented by a retaining wall, sandbags, or other filler material. For a waterproof channel, use either a flexible liner, freeform concrete, a fiberglass shell or series of spill pans, or a combination of the above. The team of plastic liner and concrete is favored by many pros. If shotcrete or gunite (see page 72) is the choice, it can often be applied at the same time the adjacent pool is built.

You can apply concrete over chicken wire backing only, but a standard 12-inch grid of 3/8- or 1/2-inch reinforcing rod is better. Before pouring the falls, however, you'll need to place the primary rocks.

Building the channel. The toughest part of the whole project is getting any big boulders into place, and you may need help. If you're using a flexible liner, position these rocks carefully, making sure not to damage or displace the liner. If the rocks are outside the liner's path, dig out beds and settle them firmly in the soil. Working in manageable sections, pour 3 inches of concrete, working it up the sides of the channels and into all the nooks and crannies.

Once the concrete has set up, brush on two to three coats of cement-based waterproofing compound. You can also use hydraulic cement, designed for repair jobs, to waterproof and help shape as desired. This is the time to test for leaks.

Anatomy of a Waterfall

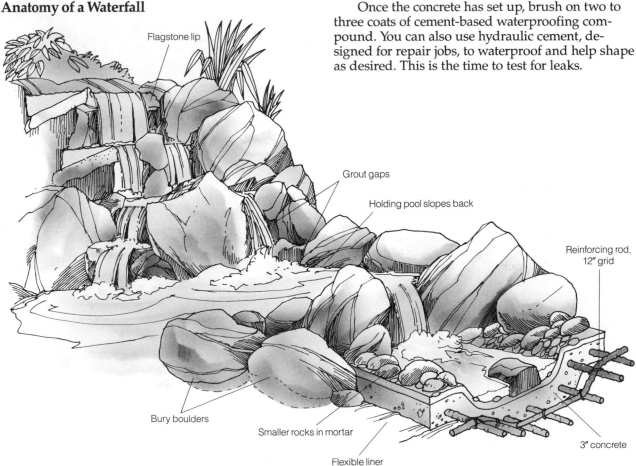

Flagstone lip

Grout gaps

Holding pool slopes back

Reinforcing rod, 12" grid

Bury boulders

Smaller rocks in mortar

Flexible liner

3" concrete

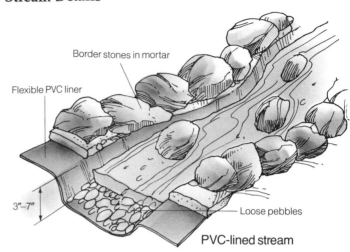

Border stones in mortar

Flexible PVC liner

3"–7"

Loose pebbles

PVC-lined stream

Adding rocks. Once the basic structure is complete, secure secondary stones, pebbles, and a flagstone or acrylic lip in a mortar bed, adding additional mix between seams to keep the water moving the way you want it to. When mortaring, concentrate on the "upstream" side, away from the main flow and main angle of view. Colored mortar—black or charcoal—blends in better than natural gray, appearing as "shadows" in the finished waterfall. Use a stiff, wet paintbrush for final troweling—it's easier to get into tight corners than a regular trowel.

Also add loose rocks or pebbles at this point to accent visually or form ripple patterns. To secure the border plantings, pack soil into the areas behind the boulders.

Streams

Streams share many construction details with both waterfalls and pools—in fact, they typically begin with a small falls and end in a holding pool.

To plan a stream, lay out a rope in the general course you want the stream to take. Be sure the proposed channel can handle the maximum flow from your pump (see page 80), plus some additional natural runoff. A finished depth of 3 to 7 inches works well: anything deeper than that requires a lot of water. The slope should be mild; a series of weirs, joined by small dammed cascades, keeps water from running off too quickly and retains some when the pump is switched off.

Stream materials include flexible liners, freeform concrete, and shotcrete or gunite. Plastic lining (see drawing at top right) may require some careful seamwork, but it's a fast way to create a waterproof membrane and is easy to camouflage.

Freeform concrete lends itself to simple "scooped out" stream designs, as the small channel serves as the form. Lay down 2 inches of 3/4-inch crushed rock, apply a layer of fine gravel, and cover with chicken wire. Pour 2 inches of concrete, working it into the base rocks or wire and troweling it up the sides. If you want to leave bare concrete for the bed, roughen the surface with a stiff broom after it has started to set up. Place any large boulders before the pour, adding smaller stones with mortar or leaving them loose.

The "dry streambed" is an effective option for a natural landscape, as well as for a drainage channel for seasonal runoff. You won't need a liner, just some perforated drain pipe to channel the water, mixed rocks and pebbles, and selected border plantings. A 2 percent grade is about right.

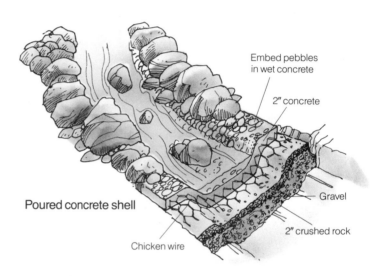

Embed pebbles in wet concrete

2" concrete

Poured concrete shell

Gravel

2" crushed rock

Chicken wire

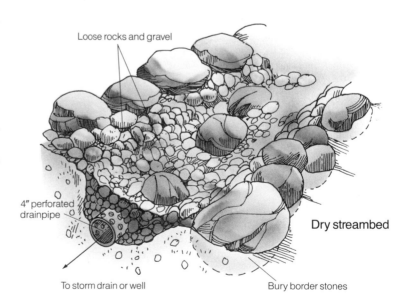

Loose rocks and gravel

4" perforated drainpipe

To storm drain or well

Dry streambed

Bury border stones

POOL PLUMBING

Pumps and plumbing for garden pools have been improved to the point where the weekend warrior can install them without much trouble. Some pools won't need plumbing at all—or at most a small submersible pump to drive a fountain jet. Larger structures, such as those including a waterfall or stream, require more elaborate plumbing systems. Accessories such as skimmers, float valves, or separate biological filters have requirements all their own. Here's a rundown on choosing a pump and using pipes, fittings, and accessories. For a look at six sample plumbing systems, see pages 84–85.

Choosing the Pump

The mechanical heart of a fountain or waterfall, the pump is merely a set of whirling blades through which the water passes and by which it is pressurized into further motion.

Submersible pumps simplify plumbing to the extreme. They sit on the floor of the pool, often hidden only by the water itself, and operate silently, one advantage over other pumps. Flexible tubing or rigid pipe (see facing page) carries water to the fountain or waterfall. Fill and drain piping, if any, are separate.

A recirculating pump is frequently the answer when the pump must be operated continuously or when water has a long distance to go from pump to outlet—often the case with waterfalls or streams. Some models are self-priming, but many are not and need to be installed in a flooded position (below water level) to retain their prime.

What size do you need? All manufacturers give electrical specifications—amps, watts, and horsepower—for their products, which are important because they measure how much electricity will be used to do the job. But the practical measure of a pump's performance is its head, the volume of water it will pump vertically, telling you how many gallons an hour a pump can deliver at a given height.

The performance specifications for a submersible pump may look like this:

Model	Gallons per hour					Amps	Watts	HP
	1 ft.	3 ft.	5 ft.	9 ft.	13 ft.			
0000	500	420	335	275	225	1.9	210	1/15

Fountain spray jets are usually designed for a specific pressure, but waterfalls and streams are more subjective. To choose a pump for a small water feature, measure the vertical distance from the water

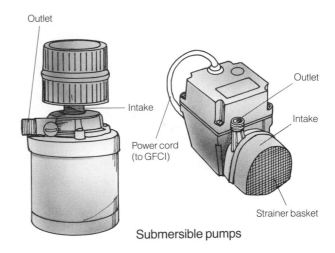

Submersible pumps

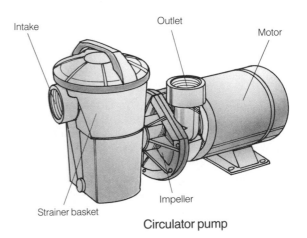

Circulator pump

level to the top of the stream or waterfall. Then, using a garden hose, start a flow of water from the top that approximates the volume of water you want. Collect this water in a 5-gallon bucket for a specified time (30 seconds or a minute), multiply the results to get gallons per hour, and compare that figure with the manufacturer's performance data.

When sizing a pump for a large system, it's best to hook up a temporary pump to a 1-1/2-inch hose or the finished plumbing. Your pump should be able to recycle an adequate flow to any filter system, so figure in this load as well.

Locating your pump. In most cases, install the pump to keep the distance it has to move the water as short as possible. For example, a waterfall pump is usually situated right at the base of the falls. The one exception is when the pump's primary function is to drive a filter: in this case, position the intake

Pipes & Fittings

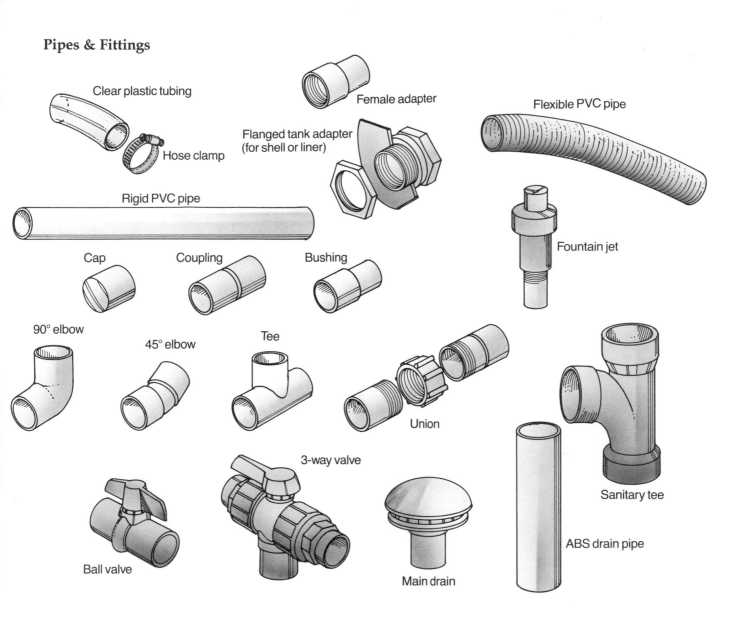

Clear plastic tubing

Hose clamp

Female adapter

Flanged tank adapter
(for shell or liner)

Flexible PVC pipe

Rigid PVC pipe

Fountain jet

Cap Coupling Bushing

90° elbow

45° elbow

Tee

Union

Sanitary tee

3-way valve

Ball valve

Main drain

ABS drain pipe

pipe—and the pump—at the opposite end of the pool to provide maximum circulation.

Elevate a submersible pump on bricks at the bottom of the pool to keep it free from silt and other pool debris. Alternatively, you may wish to form a small gravel-lined pump vault at the bottom of the pool, covering the opening with removable wire mesh. Always place some type of strainer in front of the pump to filter the worst dirt and leaves. (Many pumps include a built-in strainer.)

Ideally, a recirculating pump should be housed in a lidded 3 by 5 vault—cast in concrete or built from wood—to protect it and to eliminate clutter. You can camouflage the vault with plants or hide it behind a retaining wall.

Before placing your pump, consider how you'll supply electricity to power it. For options and details, see pages 86–89.

Pipefitting for Pools

Below you'll find a quick overview of pipes and pipefitting techniques; for help with materials, tools, and techniques, contact a plumbing equipment supplier or a professional plumber.

Pipes and fittings. The drawing above shows a sampling of popular pipes and fittings, allowing you to change direction, join pipe runs, change from plastic to copper or galvanized steel, go up or down in size, and change from a screw-on fitting to a push-in fitting. Pipes and fittings for garden pool pumps should be of plastic, copper, or galvanized steel, although on a very small pump, rubber or clear plastic tubing can be substituted for any pipe.

Whenever possible, opt for plastic pipe and fittings for both water supply and drain lines: plastic is easy to cut, is straightforward to assemble, and

A LOOK AT

BIOLOGICAL FILTERS

Biological filters use friendly bacteria to convert ammonia and nitrites in the pool water to nitrates and thus continue the purifying nitrogen cycle (see page 59). The key to designing a biological system is creating a sand, gravel, or synthetic media bed which the bacteria can call home, and pumping a steady flow of pool water through the filter media via a constantly operating pump.

Location. You can situate a biological filter at the bottom of the pool or in a remote location, connected by intake and outlet pipes. The remote tank is preferable (it's easier to maintain) but requires extra space and expense.

A concrete pool with built-in "false bottom" is ideal for an in-pool system; large, deep fiberglass shells are also relatively easy to retrofit. Fiberglass is the typical solution for a remote holding tank—it's easy to set up and drill for fittings. Even plastic industrial drums will work. The drawings on page 85 show both in-pool and remote setups.

Design. As shown below left, the biological filter is basically a 12- to 24-inch-deep media bed with an open space below, allowing the water to enter and exit at a leisurely pace. Water can travel up or down through the filter bed. Coarse aquarium sand is a traditional media choice, though fiber padding, ceramic beds, and other experimental materials are being used.

What's the best size for your biological filter? Ideally, it should be as large as the pool itself, but the filter can be much smaller—you'll just need to maintain it more intensely. The average size is 3 by 6 feet.

It takes up to 8 weeks for a bacterial colony to accumulate naturally, but you can speed up the process by "seeding" the filter with a shovelful of material from a friend's media bed.

Pump and hardware. Generally, garden pool designers figure that the pump should turn over 1 to 2 gallons per minute per square foot of filter bed surface. In practical terms, that means that the typical 3- by 6-foot biological filter will require 18 to 24 gallons per minute, or 1080 to 1440 gallons per hour. A recirculating pump is best, as the filter must operate 24 hours a day. As the filter media can die in as little as 6 to 8 hours without oxygen, you may wish to install a small air pump in case of emergencies.

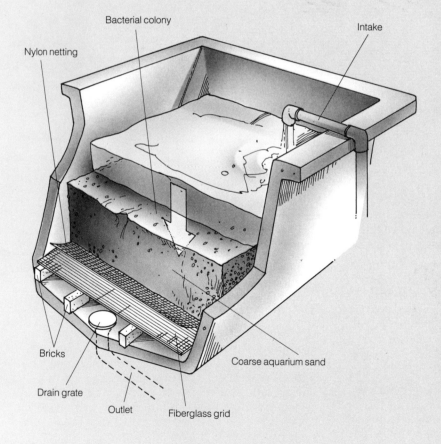

Bacterial colony

Nylon netting

Intake

Bricks

Drain grate

Outlet

Fiberglass grid

Coarse aquarium sand

won't corrode like copper or galvanized. Rigid Schedule 40 PVC is the standby, though flexible PVC, available in many areas, fits around corners without fittings and helps you ease a fiberglass pool into place. ABS plastic can be substituted for PVC for larger drain lines. Consider 1-1/2 inch pipe and fittings the norm for garden pool systems; large volumes of water may require 2-inch lines.

Working with plastic pipe. Although you can cut PVC plastic pipe with a hacksaw, a pipe cutter or power miter saw make the cleanest, squarest cuts, which helps prevent leaks.

The techniques for connecting PVC pipe and fittings are shown at right. Before you cut the pipe, be sure that measurements are exact and that you've allowed for the distance the pipe will extend into the fitting. Are you sure you have the right solvent cement for the kind of plastic you're using? Some pipes also require a primer before cementing. After joining pipe and fitting, hold them together for a minute; wait at least 6 hours before allowing water to run through the pipe.

To make a watertight seal with screw-on fittings, first wrap nylon pipe tape around the threads of the pipe.

Valves. Valves allow you to control the flow to a fountain or waterfall, divert water to a nearby drain, or shut the entire system down for repairs or maintenance.

A gate valve is handy for simple on/off use, and for isolating a pump, filter, or drain line. Need to keep water flowing in one direction, or maintain a pump's prime? Install a check valve. To control flow, opt for a ball valve, as shown on page 81. A 3-way valve allows you to shut off the flow, send a controlled flow to a fountain head, or open up a line for draining the pool.

Drains. A small pool or fountain may not need a drain, especially if it has a submersible pump that can double as a sump pump. Larger pools, however, should have a main drain to allow the pool to be drained for maintenance or emergency repairs.

Drains come in a variety of shapes and sizes; swimming pool and spa suppliers are good bets for places to look for them. You won't need an anti-vortex attachment as on a swimming pool, but you will need some type of cap or screen to keep leaves, dirt, and even fish out of the drain. Special flanged fittings are made for liners and fiberglass shells to ensure a tight seal where the drain or pipe has penetrated the liner or shell material. An example is shown on page 81. Slope the pool floor slightly toward the drain.

PVC Pipefitting

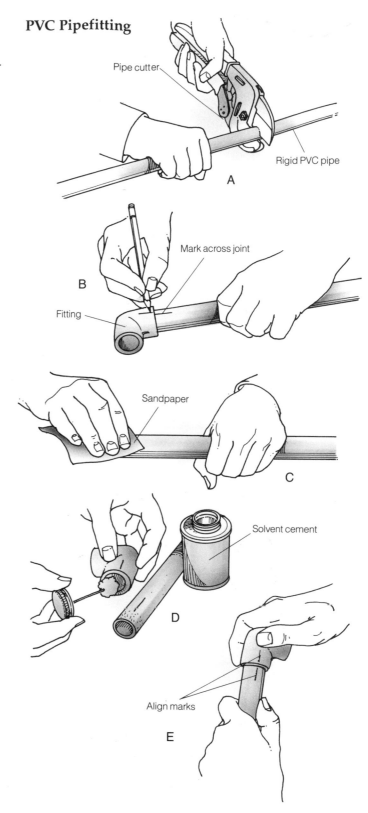

Leakproof pipefitting begins with a PVC pipe cutter (A); remove any burrs formed on the inside surface. Dry-fit pipe and fitting and mark the proper angle (B). The pipe may need light sanding or priming (C); then PVC solvent cement is brushed on both pipe and fitting (D). Join parts (E), quickly twist one-half turn, and align the marks.

To install a border drain, use perforated drain pipe and run it to a low spot in the yard, a dry well, or simply to a nearby storm drain if allowed. Dig a 12-inch-deep ditch for the drain line and line it with gravel. A minimum slope of 1/4-inch per running foot is required. A simple PVC overflow pipe can maintain pool level.

Plumbing for Pool Accessories

Fountains, filters, skimmers, and float valves all require plumbing hookups. Here are installation guidelines; for a closer look, see the drawings at right.

Fountains. Though some spray fountains come as complete units, others include the spray jet only, requiring a riser pipe—or a series of nipples and adapters—to achieve the proper height. If required, fasten the riser tightly to a stake or support block, then screw the jet onto the riser's threads.

Typically, a spill or wall fountain has no jet, simply one or more pipe ends flush with the back wall. An example is shown at bottom right. Cover the pipe end with a decorative nozzle or figurine, or hide it between masonry units, leaving a narrow slot in mortar or grout. A ball or 3-way valve maintains the flow to any fountain.

Filters. Filters—whether cartridge, pressurized-sand, or biological—require intake and outlet plumbing; a biological filter may also require custom internal parts (see "Biological Filters" on page 82). Always position the filter on the outlet side of the pump, unless you're using a separate pump and plumbing route just for the filter, which is a good idea for large pools. A separate ball valve on this line is handy.

Skimmer. A surface skimmer connected to the pump intake pulls dirt, pollen, floating algae, and leaves into the filtration system. The typical skimmer is poured in place on the side of a concrete pool, though units that hang on the side of the pool are also available.

The skimmer is most effective when it is located on the down-wind side of the pool; the wind helps the pump by pushing debris toward the opening.

Float valve. To automatically top up water lost to evaporation and splash, a float valve can do the trick. You'll need access to a nearby cold water pipe, plus a fitting or two to make the hookup.

A float valve can be located in the holding pool of a wall fountain, a niche in a pool's rock edging, or a separate, lidded chamber near the main pool.

Sample Plumbing Designs

PVC liner with spray fountain

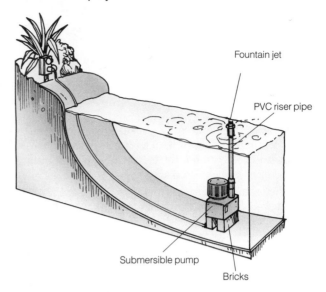

Fountain jet

PVC riser pipe

Submersible pump

Bricks

Fiberglass shell with waterfall

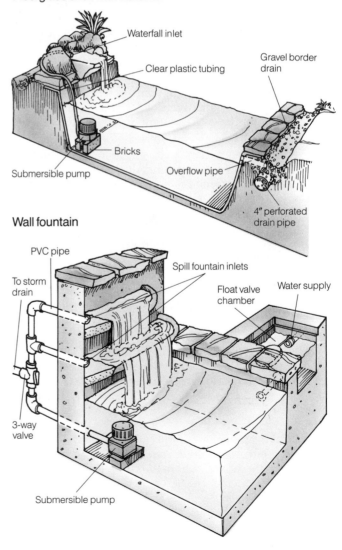

Waterfall inlet

Clear plastic tubing

Gravel border drain

Bricks

Submersible pump

Overflow pipe

4" perforated drain pipe

Wall fountain

PVC pipe

To storm drain

Spill fountain inlets

Float valve chamber

Water supply

3-way valve

Submersible pump

Freeform concrete stream

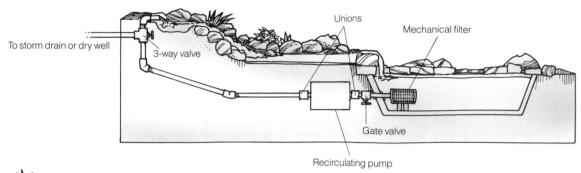

To storm drain or dry well

3-way valve

Unions

Mechanical filter

Gate valve

Recirculating pump

Split-level pools with biological filter

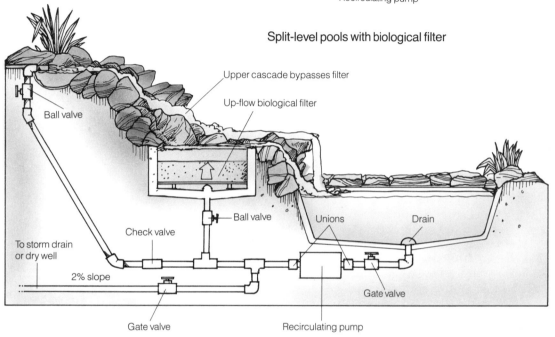

Ball valve

Upper cascade bypasses filter

Up-flow biological filter

Ball valve

Check valve

Unions

Drain

To storm drain or dry well

2% slope

Gate valve

Gate valve

Recirculating pump

Koi pond with biological filter & pressurized-sand filter

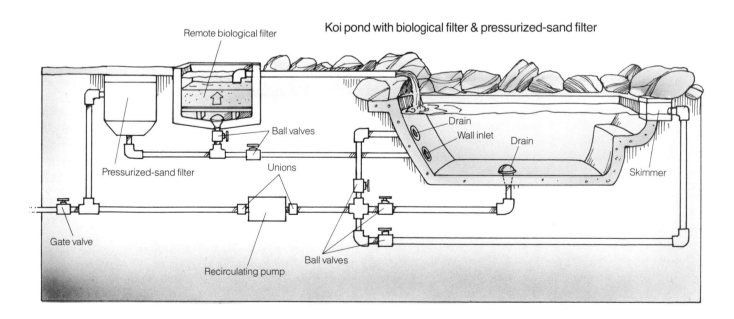

Remote biological filter

Ball valves

Drain

Wall inlet

Drain

Pressurized-sand filter

Unions

Skimmer

Gate valve

Recirculating pump

Ball valves

OUTDOOR WIRING & LIGHTING

For powering a submersible pump, accenting plants and fish, or illuminating paths, electricity is a welcome addition to any garden pool environment. You can extend your home's 120-volt system into the garden to power a pump or permanently placed light fixtures, or you can step the system down to 12 volts and use lighter-weight fixtures that can be easily moved.

A 12-volt installation is simple: cable can lie on top of the ground, perhaps hidden by foliage, or in a narrow trench, where there is much less danger that people or pets will suffer a harmful shock. In most areas, no electrical permit is required for installing a system that extends from a low-voltage plug-in transformer (the most common kind).

For brighter lighting, pumps, and other pool accessories, 120-volt wiring packs a bigger punch—and requires both buried cable and an electrical permit; code restrictions are particularly strict for installations near to and in the pool. (If you're planning a 220-volt installation for a heavy-duty recirculating pump, be sure to hire a professional.)

Before adding on to an existing circuit, add up the watts marked on the bulbs and appliances fed by that circuit. A 15-amp circuit can handle a continuous load of 1440 watts; a 20-amp circuit is rated for 1920 watts. The number of watts you can add is the difference between these figures and your total.

In purchasing light fixtures for above-water installation, be sure to get weather-resistant materials (aluminum, brass, copper, stainless steel, hard-finish plastics, ceramic clays). For underwater installation—whether fixtures are cast into the pool shell or portable—use only UL-approved types. Underwater is no place to have short circuits.

Here's the most important rule for all do-it-yourself electricians: *Never work on any "live" circuit, fixture, receptacle, or switch.* Your life may depend on it. If fuses protect your circuits, remove the appropriate fuse and take it with you. In a panel or subpanel equipped with circuit breakers, switch the appropriate breaker to the OFF position to disconnect the circuit, then tape over the switch for extra safety. If you need help to add a new circuit or you have any doubts about how to hook up to an existing one, consult an electrician.

Adding a 120-volt System

To install a 120-volt outdoor system, you may need housing boxes, a ground fault circuit interrupter (abbreviated GFCI or GFI), a set of light fixtures, and weatherproof 120-volt cable or conduit. You may also want to add an indoor switch and timer.

Choosing housing boxes. Outdoor boxes come in two types: so-called "driptight" boxes that seal vertically against falling water and "watertight" ones that seal against water coming from any direction. Unless you can ensure protection from rain, sprinklers, and even the garden hose, it's best to choose watertight boxes.

Wiring a GFCI. Even though you may plan to plug your pump or pool light into an existing outdoor receptacle, seriously consider replacing the outlet with one that has a built-in GFCI. This device works like a standard receptacle but cuts off power within 1/40 of a second if current begins leaking anywhere along the circuit.

Spotlight on Outdoor Fixtures

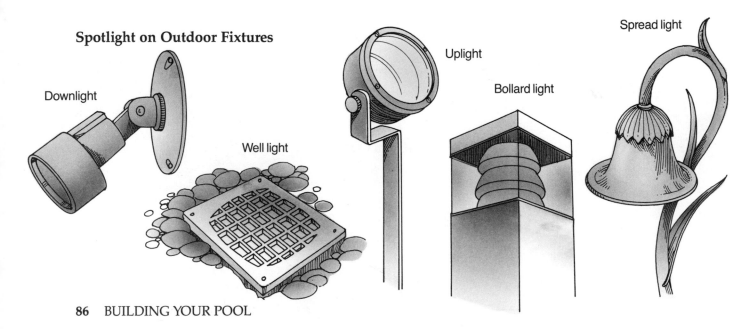

Downlight

Well light

Uplight

Spread light

Bollard light

Wiring an Indoor Switch & Power Source to New GFCI

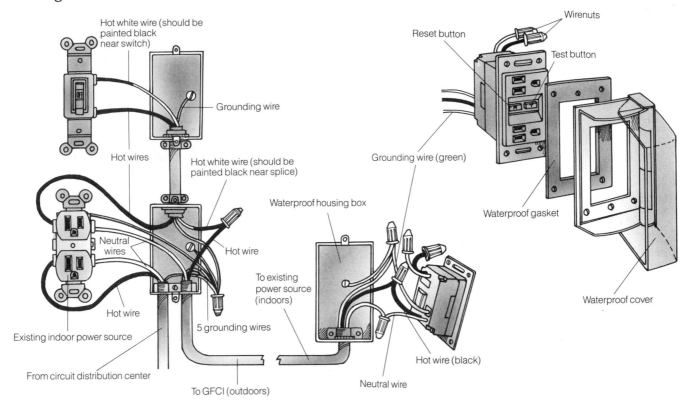

Hot white wire (should be painted black near switch)

Grounding wire

Hot wires

Hot white wire (should be painted black near splice)

Hot wire

Neutral wires

Waterproof housing box

Hot wire

To existing power source (indoors)

Existing indoor power source

5 grounding wires

From circuit distribution center

To GFCI (outdoors)

Neutral wire

Hot wire (black)

Reset button

Wirenuts

Test button

Grounding wire (green)

Waterproof gasket

Waterproof cover

The drawing above shows how to wire an outdoor GFCI. Make the connections with plastic wirenuts, following this sequence: (1) Strip 1 inch of insulation from the wire ends, and twist the ends clockwise 1-1/2 turns; (2) Snip 3/8 to 1/2 inch off the twisted wires; (3) Screw the wirenut clockwise onto the wires. Twist a short "jumper" wire from the box's grounding screw together with the other two grounding wires.

If this is the "end of the run," snip off the remaining outgoing wires from the GFCI and cover them with wirenuts as shown.

Dimmer switches allow you to set light fixtures at any level from a soft glow to full-throttle. Most dimmers can be wired in the same manner as the switch shown above. Use this setup for lights only—you won't want a dimmer-controlled pump!

Tapping a power source. Extending an inside power source to the outside is the same as extending wiring inside. You can tap into most switch, receptacle, fixture, or junction boxes as long as the box contains a neutral (white) wire and is not switch-controlled.

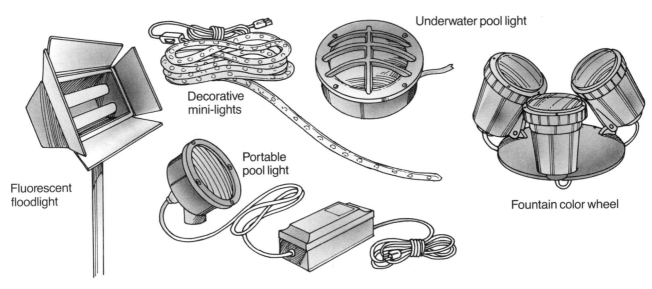

Fluorescent floodlight

Decorative mini-lights

Underwater pool light

Portable pool light

Fountain color wheel

Wiring an Indoor Switch & Timer

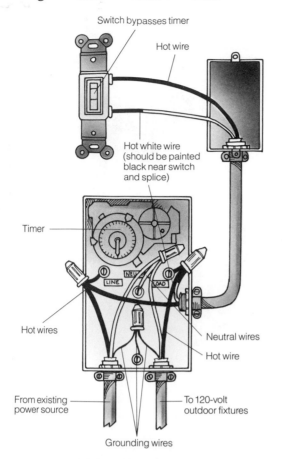

Switch bypasses timer

Hot wire

Hot white wire (should be painted black near switch and splice)

Timer

Hot wires

Neutral wires

Hot wire

From existing power source

To 120-volt outdoor fixtures

Grounding wires

Wiring 120-volt Fixtures

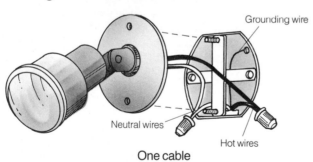

Grounding wire

Neutral wires

Hot wires

One cable

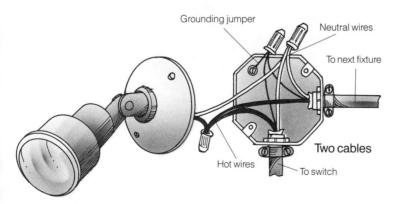

Grounding jumper

Neutral wires

To next fixture

Hot wires

To switch

Two cables

One simple method is to install an outdoor box back-to-back with an existing indoor box. Pull the indoor device from its box, remove a knockout, drill a hole through the house siding, and screw the new box in place. Then feed nonmetallic sheathed cable (NM) through the hole, leaving 8 inches of cable on each side. CAUTION: Be sure to shut off power to the circuit before beginning work.

It's also easy to add a watertight extender ring to an existing outdoor box—or even a porch light—and run new wire from there.

Installing an indoor switch and timer. By wiring in a switch and timer as shown in the drawing at left, you can turn the pump or lights on and off by hand or let the timer do it for you.

Choosing types of cable and conduit. The size wire that you must use depends on the total wattage ratings of the lighting fixtures you'll connnect to the system. Here are the maximum ratings for some typical wire sizes:

#14 wire—1440 watts at 120 volts

#12 wire—1920 watts at 120 volts

#10 wire—2880 watts at 120 volts

Many electrical codes require the use of rigid conduit for outdoor lighting. Plastic conduit, though lighter and less expensive than steel, must lie at least 18 inches underground. Steel conduit, on the other hand, can be as little as 6 inches underground. Run two thermoplastic-insulated wires (TW) through steel conduit, which is self-grounding; run three TW wires (including a ground wire) through plastic.

Some codes allow the use of flexible three-wire underground feeder cable (UF) instead of rigid conduit; the cable must be buried at least 18 inches deep. Work with UF cable in the same way you'd work with NM cable. Before covering the cable with dirt, lay a redwood board on top of it so you won't accidentally spade through it at a later time.

For details about working with conduit and cable, as well as more information on installing an outdoor electrical system, consult an electrical materials supplier or an electrician.

Hooking up the fixtures. Unless your new fixture includes a cover plate for wire connections, you'll need to furnish an accessible watertight box nearby. In most locales, metal conduit is required between the fixture and the ground.

Fixture installation varies according to type and style, so be sure to follow the manufacturer's instructions carefully. The drawing at left shows two typical arrangements.

Adding 12-volt Lighting

To install a 12-volt system, you'll need a transformer, some two-wire outdoor cable, and a set of 12-volt fixtures. To activate the system, you connect the transformer, and perhaps a separate switching device, to an existing power source.

Choosing wire thickness. Most low-voltage outdoor fixtures use stranded wire cable, the size of the wires in the cable depending on the aggregate wattage of the fixtures to be served. Here are the appropriate sizes for some typical wattages:

> #14 wire—up to 144 watts at 12 volts
>
> #12 wire—up to 192 watts at 12 volts
>
> #10 wire—up to 288 watts at 12 volts

Installing a transformer. Most transformers for outdoor lights are encased in watertight boxes, but to be safe, plan to install yours in a sheltered location at least a foot off the ground.

If you don't already have an outlet into which to plug the transformer, use an outlet equipped with a ground fault circuit interrupter (GFCI).

Though many transformers have built-in switches, some do not, in which case installing a separate switch indoors will probably prove more convenient than installing it outside.

Most transformers for home use are rated from 100 to 300 watts, which shows the total allowable wattage of the fixtures serviced. The higher the rating, the more lengths of 100-foot cable—up to a total of four—the transformer can supply power through; each length extends like a spoke from the transformer.

To connect one or more low-voltage cables to the transformer, simply wrap the bare wire ends of each cable clockwise around the screw terminals on the transformer and tighten the terminals.

Connecting fixtures to the cable. Once the transformer is in place and you've decided where to put the fixtures, you'll need to hook them into the cable or cables leading from the transformer.

With some fixtures, pierce the cable with a screw-down connector already attached to the back of the fixture. With others, you must screw an unattached connector to the main cable and to the end of a short cable leading from the fixture. Neither of these types of connector requires removing insulation from the cable.

A few fixture brands require splicing into the main cable with wirenuts. For these, use plastic housing boxes to insulate splices that can't be pushed back into the fixtures.

Wiring 12-volt Fixtures

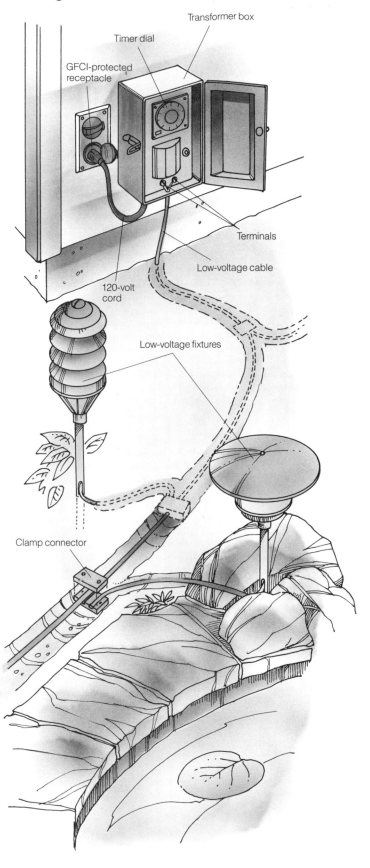

Transformer box

Timer dial

GFCI-protected receptacle

Terminals

Low-voltage cable

120-volt cord

Low-voltage fixtures

Clamp connector

MAINTAINING YOUR POOL

Once your garden pool is installed, you'll want to embark on a careful maintenance program to keep it in top shape. The following pages are intended as a quick reference guide to common procedures, problems, and their remedies. In addition, always read and follow the manufacturer's instructions in the owner's manuals for your pool hardware.

Maintaining a pool requires very few pieces of equipment. A hose-powered pool vacuum (see the drawing below), a leaf skimmer, and nylon-bristled brushes are the basic units. Aluminum handles that fit the vacuum cleaner, leaf skimmer, and brushes are available in lengths from 8 to 16 feet. You may choose from a wide variety of other accessories, but nothing more is really necessary.

Pool Cleaning Procedure

Although a properly balanced pool should keep itself in working condition for long periods at a stretch, an occasional draining and cleaning may be required.

Generally, fall and spring are the two best times for a pool-cleaning project. In fall, leaves have freshly fallen and you can extract them before they rot on the pool bottom, robbing plants and fish of oxygen. Also, it's the time to bring in tender water plants for the winter months (see page 94 for details) and to trim back dead stems and leaves. But spring is good too, just as the water warms up, plant life takes off, and fish are once again active and feeding. "Spring cleaning" is an especially apt term for fish ponds, as that's the time that fish diseases tend to swing into high gear.

If you've installed a main drain, it's easy to empty the pool; otherwise, drain it with a pump, or use a hose as a siphon to drain the water to a nearby low-lying area. Remove the bottom sediment and leaves, being careful not to damage a liner or shell.

If you have fish, remove them from the pool: drain the water part of the way down, then net the fish and move them to a shaded fiberglass holding tank, a large aquarium, or a large plastic garbage can filled with water. Shade the temporary container and, if possible, add some aeration in the form of a pool pump or at least a small aquarium aerator.

Carefully inspect the pool shell or liner, especially if you suspect leaks. Obviously, this is the time to correct any problems (see "Pool Repairs," pages 92–93).

To clean pool walls and bottom, simply spray them with a strong jet from your garden hose; then drain the pool once more before refilling it. Always use restraint when cleaning—strong scrubbing or scraping can remove all beneficial bacteria from the pool.

Refurbishing a concrete garden pool is a little more involved. First drain the pool. Scrub the sides (including tile) and bottom with a long-handled, stiff-bristled brush dipped in a solution of one part muriatic acid and one part water. Use this with caution, it's caustic; you'll need rubber gloves and eye protection. Rinse the pool with a strong jet from the garden hose and let it dry for 1 to 2 days; then wash it again with a solution of trisodium phosphate (dissolve according to label instructions). Rinse again with water and allow the pool to dry overnight.

Maintenance Tools & Accessories

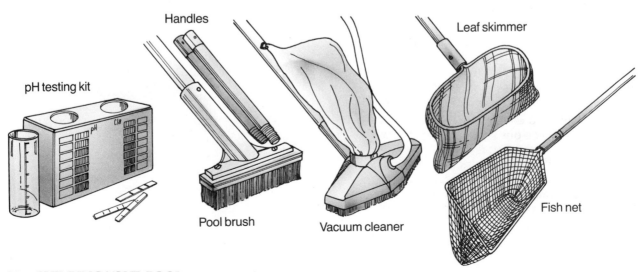

pH testing kit

Handles

Pool brush

Vacuum cleaner

Leaf skimmer

Fish net

To paint the pool surface, use a special epoxy or rubber-base paint (available in many colors). Brush or roll on the first coat, let it dry for 2 days, and apply a second coat. A gallon covers about 250 square feet. Before refilling the pool, let the paint dry for 14 days. Paint lasts 4 to 6 years if you keep the water clean.

Water Chemistry

Water chemistry in a garden pool refers to the balancing of several factors critical to water quality and the happiness of any water plants or fish. Measure the pH, or potential hydrogen, of your pool water before introducing plants or fish, and on a regular basis thereafter, which tells you where the water is on the acidity/alkalinity scale. On a logarithmic scale of 0 (total acidity) to 14 (total alkalinity), the ideal pH range for a garden pool is 6.8 to 7.6.

Soda ash or sodium bicarbonate raises the pH; phosphoric acid, sodium bisulfate, or vinegar will lower it. Most of these products are available under simpler proprietary names. A test kit that shows acid and alkali demand helps determine how much of either acid or alkali to add to the water. With some kits, you test the water by adding a reagent, in liquid or tablet form, to a precise amount of pool water contained in a device called a test block; comparing the resulting color variations with those shown on the test block tells what chemicals are needed. Other kits use paper strips that change color when dipped into the pool water. Again, the resulting hue is compared with a printed chart for interpretation. Test kit reagents must be fresh; throw them away once they're over 12 months old.

In addition to pH testing, you should test a fish pond for ammonia and nitrite levels. In light of the nitrogen cycle (see page 59), concentrations of both ammonia and nitrites should be as low as possible. You can buy separate test kits to monitor these factors, or a multi-test kit that measures pH, ammonia, and nitrites. To alter either ammonia or nitrites, small water changes are necessary until the levels come down to undetectable levels.

Both chlorine and chloramines are toxic to fish. Chlorine will dissipate out of standing water in a few days, but you'll need to take chemical steps if your water supply has chloramines added to it. Proprietary chemicals are available for dealing with both chlorine and chloramines; even small amounts of water for "topping up" must be treated in problem areas.

CALCULATING POOL VOLUME

Prescribing a pump, a filter, water treatment, or fish medication all hinge on a working knowledge of your pool's capacity in gallons. Generally, to find a pool's volume first calculate its area, which corresponds to the length times the width, then multiply the area by the average depth and a conversion factor (7.5). The trick is finding the "length and width" of an informal pool! If you can't find a shape below that approximates your pool, divide the outline up into units of simpler shapes, figure the volume of each chunk, and add them together for the total.

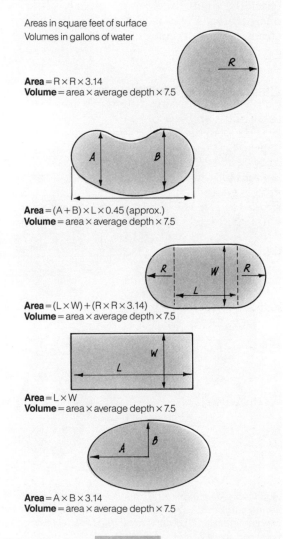

Areas in square feet of surface
Volumes in gallons of water

Area = R × R × 3.14
Volume = area × average depth × 7.5

Area = (A + B) × L × 0.45 (approx.)
Volume = area × average depth × 7.5

Area = (L × W) + (R × R × 3.14)
Volume = area × average depth × 7.5

Area = L × W
Volume = area × average depth × 7.5

Area = A × B × 3.14
Volume = area × average depth × 7.5

Maintaining Pool Hardware

The owner's manual for your pump outlines the maintenance the equipment requires. Usually, you'll only need to clean the debris from the strainer basket. To remove the basket, shut off the pump; if the pump is below water level, turn off any valves. Then take off the cover, lift out the basket, and either clean it or replace it with a spare. Though most pumps are self-priming, they may lose prime when the basket is removed. To prime the pump, take off the basket cover, start the pump, and within a few seconds it should be pumping water free of air bubbles. If not, try the priming procedure one more time. Running a pump dry or with air entering the system can overheat and do serious damage to both pump and motor. Inspect pump and filter once a month, or whenever you notice the water getting dirty.

If a submersible pump is causing problems, check the volute (intake pipe), which is held on by a few screws. Clean it, and the impeller, with a strong jet of water and reassemble the pieces.

To clean a cartridge filter, just remove the cartridge and hose it off, directing the water at an angle to the cartridge to remove the dirt. Return it to the housing, replace the cover and seal it, and restart the system.

A biological filter's media bed requires a light raking about once a month to remove accumulated debris. About twice a year, you'll need to either vacuum or backflush the system to get rid of excess sludge and sediments. A properly sized and maintained media bed should last several years.

A pressurized-sand filter needs more frequent backwashing. The filter has a valve, either slide or rotary, that controls the flow of water. If you must backwash your filter often and notice debris in the pool, open the filter and check the condition of the bed. If you find caked dirt in the sand, it's time to replace the sand.

Pool Repairs

Flexible liners, fiberglass shells, and concrete may develop cracks or leaks due to an accident or just

Cleaning Pump & Filter

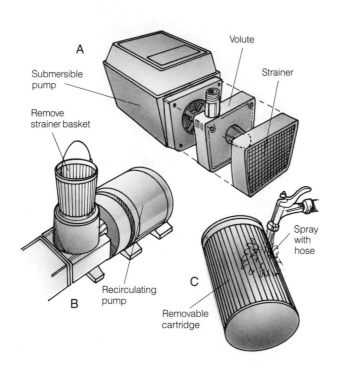

A submersible pump's intake may clog: to clean, remove the strainer and volute (A). Empty a recirculating pump's strainer basket regularly (B). Filters need attention, too: a cartridge filter requires a regular hosing down (C).

Repairing a PVC Liner

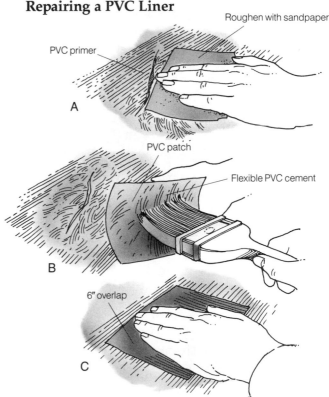

To repair the typical flexible liner, first prime and sand the damaged area (A), apply PVC solvent cement to both liner and patch (B), and smooth the patch firmly into place (C). If possible, weight the patch until it dries.

eventual wear and tear. Here's how to attack the problems.

Repairing a flexible liner. PVC and most other flexible liners can be repaired by patching with scraps of the original liner (see drawing on facing page); use the adhesive available from the manufacturer as recommended. Patch butyl-rubber liners with the 4-inch tape and adhesive made for joining seams.

Fiberglass repairs. Gelcoat deterioration detracts from the pool's appearance but rarely constitutes a serious problem. To repair a crack, use a standard fiberglass repair kit, containing sections of fiberglass and a two-part epoxy adhesive consisting of resin and hardener. If serious cracks are evident, you have an improperly supported shell; drain the pool and check its structural support.

A coat of epoxy paint improves the appearance of an older fiberglass pool. Be sure to follow the recommendation of the paint manufacturer; preparing the surface properly before painting is essential if the paint is to adhere.

Concrete repairs. Masonry sealers, primarily of Portland cement, chemical combinations, or both, will stop seepage through minor cracks and crazing. Most require a clean pool surface and two coats.

Portland cement—or hydraulic patching mixtures containing Portland cement—can be pressed into a crack after enlarging it with a cold chisel (see drawing below). Again, follow the instructions provided by the manufacturer. Several quick-drying compounds are formulated for making repairs underwater.

If your concrete pool has deteriorated to the point where it needs major repairs, you may want to consider installing a new shell inside the old one. Treating the old pool as a big hole in the ground, you or a contractor can add new concrete, slip a fiberglass shell inside the old pool, or drape a flexible liner over the inside. You can then add new edging and borders to the pool, as well as refurbish any mechanical systems. If you must run new pipes or conduit through old concrete, bore the holes with a core drill.

Refurbishing a Concrete Pool

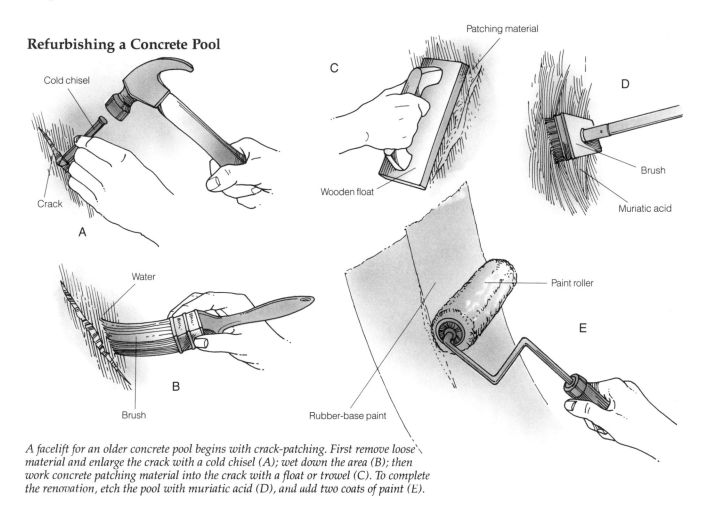

A facelift for an older concrete pool begins with crack-patching. First remove loose material and enlarge the crack with a cold chisel (A); wet down the area (B); then work concrete patching material into the crack with a float or trowel (C). To complete the renovation, etch the pool with muriatic acid (D), and add two coats of paint (E).

Fish Disease Reference Chart

Disease	Symptoms
Anchor worm Parasite	Tiny twiglike worms, up to ½ inch in length, attach themselves to skin; twin egg sacs may be visible at end.
Cloudy eye Nonspecific	As the name indicates, symptom is milky cloud over eyes; fish loses energy, appetite.
Columnarius **(mouth fungus)** Bacteria	As indicated at left, really a bacteria, not a fungus. Usually attacks head and mouth region. Contagious.
Dropsy **(pinecone** **disease)** Bacteria	Scales stand out from body as on a pinecone, hence the name. Swollen abdomen is common. Usually fatal.
Finrot/Tailrot Bacteria	Begins with light, foggy patches; progresses to bloody and rotted tail or fins. Indicative of unclean pond conditions.
Fish lice Parasite	Twin suckers attach to skin; lice are light green or brown, up to ½ inch in diameter, hard to see unaided; fish rub against pool sides and rocks in effort to "brush off" lice.
Flukes **(gill or skin)** Parasites	Fish swim with jerky motion, mouth at surface as if exhausted (if gill flukes). Fish skin appears whitish; fish attempt to rub against objects in pond (if skin flukes).
Fungus Fungus	Cotton- or wool-like appearance on body or fins. Attacks previously injured or stressed fish. May appear whitish or even greenish (mixed with algae).
Ich **(white spot)** Parasite	White spots may cover body; on close observation, "noodlelike" parasites may be visible. Fish rub against objects.
Leeches Parasite	Flattened worms, up to 1 inch long, brown or greyish in color.
Oxygen depletion Water condition	Fish mouth at surface, appear exhausted.
Ulcer **(hole-in-the-side** **disease)** Nonspecific	Ulcer appears on fish body; often fatal.

Plant Care

Remove yellowing leaves, faded flowers, and fruits periodically. Lopping shears or pole pruners are convenient tools if you have to reach far out over the water. Established plants need regular fertilizing during the growing season: feed them by burying slow-release 20-10-5 fertilizer tablets in their root zones, or by broadcasting dry pellets. (Use fertilizers with restraint in fish ponds, however.) Most water plants benefit from seasonal thinning and/or dividing.

Aphids, the commonest pest of water lilies, can usually be controlled by washing the plants with a garden hose, or if you have fish, they will soon consume the aphids. For heavier infestation, apply oil spray at growing-season strength; this will not adversely affect fish, snails, or plants. Spray on cloudy days or in the evening to prevent leaf scorch.

BT (Bacillus thuringiensis) is one insecticide safe for use near pools and is effective for combating caterpillars and other pests that feed on your marginal plants. A variety of BT is designed for eradicating mosquitos, but if you have fish, you should have no problem.

First frost marks the time to protect your hardy water plants: lower them to the bottom of the pool, cover them with plastic, or—best of all—bring the containers indoors for the winter, keeping the plants warm and moist in a snug greenhouse. Tropical water lilies and other warmth-loving plants are considered annuals in cold climates.

Caring for Fish

Fish don't ask for much, but a few basic procedures will keep them happy and healthy.

Spring cleaning. Spring is the time that water warms up and fish resume active feeding; it's also the time that fish diseases hit their stride. In this light, spring is the best time for a thorough inspection of your fish, shell or liner, and pump and filter system.

Overwintering. If your pond is 18 inches or deeper, you shouldn't have to worry about it freezing solid—especially if you keep a pump in operation. Lack of oxygen can be a problem, though; you may wish to run a small pool de-icer that keeps a small hole open to allow some air exchange. An improvised pool cover—netting and straw, canvas awning material, plastic grid and opaque sheeting—or more formal glazing can help maintain the water temperature, although a small pool heater is the premier choice.

Of course, if you have a pond or tub garden with just a few goldfish, simply move them to warmer quarters when winter winds howl.

Diseases. Most fish diseases are a result of stress, which weakens a fish's natural ability to fight off bacteria or parasites. Stressful conditions include overcrowding, rough handling and transport, insufficient oxygen, temperature swings, and toxins in the water. If pool conditions are up to par, you should have little trouble—especially after the fish have been in the pool for awhile—but make it a habit to observe your fish on a regular basis.

Fish diseases are either due to parasites, bacteria, or a fungus. To help you identify the problem, see the chart on the facing page.

Pet stores and mail-order sources sell many proprietary medications for treating fish diseases. Standard treatments for parasites include trichlorfon, and a mixture of malachite green and formalin. A variety of wide-spectrum antibiotics treat bacteria and fungus. A salt bath can help clear up many fish diseases. Mix in rock salt at the rate of 44 pounds per 1,000 gallons of pool water; or treat isolated fish for 1 hour at twice that concentration. A salt bath is a one-time proposition: salt concentrations build up in the water until flushed out.

Consult a veterinarian, koi expert, koi club, or textbook for help with any problem you don't understand. If you have a biological filter, be sure that whatever treatment you choose will not affect the bacteria in your filter media.

POOLS

BY MAIL

Flexible liners, fiberglass shells, submersible pumps, fountain jets, float valves, water lilies, oxygenating plants, fish food: here are places where you can access all the above and more. Some mail-order sources even send goldfish and koi (by express mail only, of course)! Be forewarned: these catalogs can be habit-forming.

This is only a partial listing, including a sampling of large, national mail-order sources; smaller, more regional companies, plus those specializing in water plants or koi, abound. Garden pool enthusiasts and builders can steer you to local favorites—or try a nearby koi club, a garden supplier, or the phone book.

Hermitage Garden Pools
P.O. Box 361
Canastota, NY 13032

Kingkoi International
5879 Avis Lane
Harrisburg, PA 17112

Lilypons Water Gardens
P. O. Box 10
Lilypons, MD 21717

McAllister Water Gardens
7420 St. Helena Highway
Yountville, CA 94599

Paradise Water Gardens
14 May St.
Whitman, MA 02382

Serenity Ponds & Streams
4488 Candleberry Ave.
Seal Beach, CA 90740

S. Scherer and Sons
104 Waterside Ave.
Northport, NY 11768

Slocum Water Gardens
1101 Cypress Gardens Blvd.
Winter Haven, FL 33880

Van Ness Water Gardens
2460 N. Euclid Ave.
Upland, CA 91786

Waterford Gardens
74 East Allendale Rd.
Saddle River, NJ 07458

Wicklein's Aquatic Farm & Nursery, Inc.
1820 Cromwell Bridge Rd.
Baltimore, MD 21234

INDEX